CHRISTMAS

COOKBOOK

Great Recipes for Your Christmas Dinner From Start to Finish

(From the Christmas Shortbread Cookbook to the Table)

Thomas Ellsworth

Published by Alex Howard

Christmas Cookbook: Great Recipes for Your Christmas Dinner From Start to Finish (From the Christmas Shortbread Cookbook to the Table)

ISBN 978-1-989891-96-4

Legal & Disclaimer

The information contained in this book is not designed to replace or take the place of any form of medicine or professional medical advice. The information in this book has been provided for educational and entertainment purposes only.

Table of contents

Part 1

Introduction

Whether you actually celebrate Christmas because of the religious connection, or just because it happens whatever you believe in, there is always one good reason to celebrate. The food!

There is so much more choice, and it becomes a time of year when feasting comes back into fashion and we can overcome any guilty conscience about eating heartily. This is all very well, but it is sometimes difficult to know where to start, particularly if this is your first time at playing host for the occasion.

Hopefully, you will find this little book useful. It should be able to guide you through snacks and cookies, to side dishes, main meals, desserts and finally cakes. So much choice! Traditional fayre is to be found in here, but the list is by no mean without limit. There will be more detailed or specialized books we publish in the future to try and cover everything you could need. But for now, we are sure you will find this book useful.

To get you into a Christmas mood the very first recipe is one that will produce just a seasonal smell, evoking a lot of memories for some and the sheer pleasure of association for others. Alongside the traditional Christmas cake, you will find a German Christmas cake and a Danish Christmas cake. Next to the Christmas pudding is a recipe for the sauce to accompany it. Ending with a special bonus recipe for a special cup of coffee, there should be something for everyone in here.

There are a number of recipes you would expect, and perhaps a few you would not. We are sure you will have fun exploring, not just the recipes, but your own culinary skills. However you celebrate your Christmas this year, this little book will help you enjoy it even more.

Image: FreeDigitalPhotos.net

For your convenience, to allow easy navigation throughout the book, each recipe in the Table of Contents is linked to the recipe itself. You just need to click on it to be taken straight there. The heading of each recipe in the book is also linked back to the Table of Contents.

Remember, cooking is an art, not a science. You don't have to do anything you don't want to. You need only treat each recipe as a guide. It's not compulsory to follow it. You can add ingredients, take them away, increase or decrease the quantity, change the cooking time to suit your own tastes, or do anything else with it.

In the ingredients list for each recipe we have put the ingredients in the order they appear in the recipe. Many recipes call for Canola oil. For those not in North America, where it is common, this is simply rapeseed oil. You can substitute rapeseed or any other vegetable oil for canola.

The number of suggested servings we put on each recipe is very moveable. Each of us is different. In a typical family or dinner party you might have people with a gargantuan appetite, others might be on a diet, or just have very small appetites. You know best how large or small a pie needs to be to satisfy everyone, and whether you need to add a bit to the suggested ingredients, or take some away Change what you like, when you like, and how you like, to make each meal your own. This always helps if an ingredient is not available, or too expensive. Just change it!

Now all it needs is for us to say good luck to you, and Happy Christmas.

Weights & Measures Conversion Table

For your ease of use we have taken the Metric measure above 1fl oz to the nearest 5 grams/ml.

1 ounce = 28.4 grams

1 pound = 454 grams

1 kg = 2.2 lb

1 fluid oz = 28.4 milliliters

Dry Weights

½ oz = 14g

¾ oz = 21g

1 oz = 28g

2 oz = 55g

3 oz = 85g

4oz = 115g

5 oz = 140g

6 oz = 170g

7 oz = 200g

8 oz = 225g

9 oz = 255g

10 oz = 285g

11 oz = 310g

12 oz = 340g

13 oz = 370g

14 oz = 400g

15 oz = 425g

16 oz = 455g

17 oz = 485g

18 oz = 510g

19 oz = 540g

20 oz = 570g

21 oz = 595g

22 oz = 625g

23 oz = 655g

24 oz = 680g

1½ lb = 680g

2 lb = 910g

2 lb 4 oz = 1kg

Wet Measures

1 fl oz = 28ml

2 fl oz = 55ml

3 fl oz = 85ml

4 fl oz = 110ml

5 fl oz = 140ml (¼ Pint)

6 fl oz = 170ml

7 fl oz = 200ml

8 fl oz = 225ml

9 fl oz = 255ml

10 fl oz = 285ml (½ Pint)

11 fl oz = 310ml

12 fl oz = 340ml

13 fl oz = 370ml

14 fl oz = 400ml

15 fl oz = 425ml (¾ Pint)

16 fl oz = 455ml (US Pint)

17 fl oz = 485ml

18 fl oz = 510ml

19 fl oz = 540ml

20 fl oz = 570ml (1 Pint)

40 fl oz = 1.14lt (2 Pints)

60 fl oz = 1.71lt (3 Pints)

80 fl oz = 2.28lt (4 Pints)

100 fl oz = 2.85lt (5 Pints)

Small Quantities

¼ tsp = 1.25g

½ tsp = 2.5g

¾ tsp = 3.75g

1 tsp = 5g

1tbsp = 15g

Celsius/Fahrenheit/Gas Mark

110C / 225F / Gas ¼

130C / 250F / Gas ½

140C / 275F / Gas 1

150C / 300F / Gas 2

170C / 325F / Gas 3

180C / 350F / Gas 4

190C / 375F / Gas 5

200C / 400F / Gas 6

220C / 425F / Gas 7

230C / 450F / Gas 8

240C / 475F / Gas 9

U. S. Cups

¼ Cup / 2 fl oz / 60ml

½ Cup / 4 fl oz / 115ml

1 Cup / 8 fl oz / 230ml

2 Cups / 16 fl oz (1 US Pint) 455ml

These figures are an approximation because different ingredients weigh differently for a given volume.

Note:

A pint isn't always a pint: In British, Australian, and often Canadian, recipes, you'll see an imperial pint listed as 20 fluid ounces. American and some Canadian recipes use the American pint measurement, which is 16 fluid ounces. We have used the British measurement of 20 fl oz, except in Cups, where we have used the US measure of 16 fl oz.

1 Tablespoon = .5 fluid oz or 14.79 ml

3 tsp = 1 Tablespoon

4 Tablespoons = 1/4 cup

16 Tablespoons = 1 cup

1. Holiday Spice Potpourri

For the smell of Christmas

4 lemons

4 oranges

10 crumbled bay leaves

10 broken cinnamon sticks

8 oz (225g) jelly jars with lids

½ cup allspice

½ cup whole cloves

1. Preheat the oven to 325 degrees F, 170 degrees C or Gas Mark 3.

2. Carefully peel the fruit using a vegetable peeler. Take care not to remove any of the white pith, just the peel. Cut the peel into 1 inch (25mm) strips.

3. Lay the pieces of peel on a paper towel on a baking tin and place in the oven for 1½ hours, turning occasionally.

4. Spread the pieces of peel on another paper towel and allow it to dry naturally for a further 24 hours.

5. Use a medium bowl and mix together the remaining ingredients with the pieces of peel.

6. Pour the mixture into the jars and screw the lids on tightly. The jars can be decorated to look a little more festive.

7. To use, remove the lid to scent a room or add 1 tablespoon of boiling water to a jar to release the scent.

2. Christmas Eve Cookies

Serves 4 (approx 30 cookies)

2 large egg whites

¼ tsp cream of tartar

2/3rd cup extra fine granulated sugar or caster sugar

1 cup mini chocolate chips

½ cup raisins

½ cup chopped pecans

1. Preheat the oven to 350 degrees F, 180 degrees C or Gas Mark 4.

2. Line a couple of cookie sheets with aluminum foil in preparation.

3. Beat the egg whites with a whisk, then add the cream of tartar and beat again.

4. Add the sugar and beat for 2 minutes, until thickened.

5. Gradually fold in all the remaining ingredients using a wooden spoon.

6. Drop the mixture onto the cookie sheets and place in the oven.

7. When you have closed the door turn the oven OFF and leave overnight.

8. Next day, remove the cookie sheets and peel the foil from the bottom of the cookies.

9. Store the cookies in an airtight container until used.

3. Christmas Baubles

Serves 4

1 x 14 oz (400g) can of coconut

1 can condensed milk

8 oz (225g) chopped dates

8 oz (225g) red candied cherries

8 oz (225g) green candied cherries

4 cups chopped pecans

1. Preheat the oven to 350 degrees F, 180 degrees C or Gas Mark 4.

2. Use a medium bowl and mix all the ingredients together.

3. Roll the mixture into balls.

4. Place on a baking tray and bake for 20 minutes.

5. Dust lightly with powdered sugar and they are ready to eat, hot or cold.

4. Sausage & Cheese Cookies

Serves 6

1 roll of sausage meat

1 finely chopped Spanish onion

1lb (455g) grated cheddar

3 cups Bisquick mix

¾ cup milk

1. Preheat the oven to 425 degrees f, 220 degrees C or Gas Mark 7.

2. Grease a cookie sheet in preparation.

3. Use a medium bowl and mix together the sausage meat and the chopped onion.

4. Add the cheddar, Bisquick mix, and milk, and thoroughly mix. Use a blender to finish mixing.

5. Drop the mixture onto the prepared cookie sheet using a small spoon. (You need to end up with cookie-sized circles)

6. Bake for 10 to 15 minutes until nicely brown.

7. Can be served hot or cold.

5. Fruit Shortbread Cookies

Serves 4 (36 cookies)

1 tsp baking powder

1 tsp cream of tartar

2½ cups plain flour

1½ cups confectioners' sugar

1 cup soft butter

1 egg

9 oz (255g) mincemeat

1 tsp vanilla essence

1. Preheat the oven to 375 degrees F, 190 degrees C or Gas Mark 5.

2. Use a medium bowl and mix together the baking powder, cream of tartar, and flour.

3. Use a large bowl and beat the sugar and butter until fluffed up. Add the egg and beat.

4. Gradually crumble in the mincemeat, add the vanilla essence and stir.

5. Add the dry mixture from the other bowl and mix to a stiff consistency.

6. Roll into balls about the size of a golf ball and place on a plain cookie sheet. Press down slightly to flatten.

7. Place in the oven and bake for 10 minutes or so until browned.

8. Serve with a dusting of powdered sugar.

6. Meringue Puffs

Serves 6 (24 cookies)

<u>Pastry Balls</u>

½ cup powdered (icing) sugar

½ cup butter

½ tsp vanilla essence

1 egg yolk

¼ tsp salt

1½ cups plain flour

<u>Meringue Filling</u>

1 egg white

2 tbsp sugar

½ cup finely chopped pecans

12 candied red cherries

1. Preheat the oven to 350 degrees F, 180 degrees C or Gas Mark 4.

<u>Pastry Balls</u>

2. Use a medium bowl to mix together the powdered sugar and butter until fluffed up.

3. Add the vanilla essence and the egg yolk and mix thoroughly.

4. Slowly add the salt and flour, mixing to a sturdy dough.

5. Form the dough into golf ball sized balls and set on a plain cookie sheet.

6. Use the end of the handle of a wooden spoon to make a hollow in each ball of dough for the meringue filling.

7. Chill the dough balls whilst making the meringue filling.

Meringue Filling

1a. Use a small bowl and whisk the egg white until it starts to foam. Add the sugar and continue to whisk until soft, stiff peaks form.

2a. Gently add the pecans and fold into the mixture.

3a. Use a teaspoon to spoon a generous amount of the mixture into the hollows in the dough balls.

4a. Bake in the oven for 15 minutes.

5a. Cut the candied cherries in half and place one half on the top of each meringue puff.

7. Gingerbread Men

Makes approx 20

12 oz (340g) plain flour

1 tsp baking powder

4 oz (115g) butter

5½ tsp ground ginger

1 egg

4 tbsp golden syrup

6 oz (170g) brown sugar

1½ tsp cinnamon

Gingerbread men cookie cutter!

1. Preheat the oven to 350 degrees F, 180 degrees C or Gas Mark 4.

2. Lightly grease a baking or cookie tray in preparation.

3. Use a medium bowl and use your fingers to mix together the flour, baking powder, butter, cinnamon, and ground ginger, to form a crumbly mixture.

4. Add the egg, golden syrup and sugar and mix thoroughly to get a pastry mixture.

5. Lightly dust a flat surface with flour and roll out the mixture with a rolling pin to a thickness of about ¼ inch (6mm).

6. Use the cutter to cut out the gingerbread men shapes and lay them on the baking tray.

7. Bake for 10 to 15 minutes until done. You may need to keep checking as different ovens will alter the cooking time without you realizing it.

8. Decorate with raisins or small candies for eyes and buttons as desired and allow to cool.

8. Coconut Cookies

Makes approx 24 cookies

1 cup butter

½ cup white sugar

½ cup brown sugar

1 egg

1 tsp vanilla essence

1 cup shredded coconut

2 cups plain flour

1 tsp baking powder

1 tsp cream of tartar

½ tsp salt

Granulated sugar

1. Preheat the oven to 350 degrees F, 180 degrees C or Gas Mark 4.

2. Use a medium bowl to mix together the butter with the white and brown sugars to form a creamy mixture.

3. Add the egg and vanilla essence and beat thoroughly.

4. Mix in the coconut, flour, baking powder, cream of tartar, and salt, and form a stiff pastry mix.

5. Form the pastry mix into balls from 1 teaspoon of mixture per cookie and dip in granulated sugar to give a coating. Place the coated balls on a baking or cookie tray and flatten slightly.

6. Bake in the oven for 8 to 10 minutes until done.

9. Meringue Delights

Makes 12

2 egg whites

Pinch of salt

¼ tsp cream of tartar

½ cup white sugar

½ tsp vanilla essence

4 oz (115g) chocolate chips

1. Preheat the oven to 375 degrees F, 190 degrees C or Gas Mark 5.

2. Line a baking sheet with parchment paper in preparation.

3. Use a medium whisk and whisk together the egg whites until frothy, then add the salt and cream of tartar. Continue to whisk until the mixture becomes stiff, then gradually add in the sugar, then the vanilla essence. When thoroughly mixed, gently fold in the chocolate chips.

4. Drop a heaped teaspoonful of the mixture onto the baking sheet for each cookie. Use 1 heaped teaspoonful per cookie until all the mixture is used.

5. Place the baking sheet in the oven and close the door.

6. Turn the oven off and leave the cookies in the oven for 5 hours.

10. Coffee & Walnut Chocolate Chip Cookies

Makes approx 24 cookies

12 0z (340g) chocolate chips

2 tbsp instant coffee

2 tsp boiling water

¾ tsp baking powder

½ tsp salt

1¼ cup plain flour

½ cup butter

½ cup white sugar

½ cup brown sugar

1 egg

½ cup chopped walnuts

1. Preheat the oven to 350 degrees F, 180 degrees C or Gas Mark 4.

2. Take ½ of the chocolate chips and melt over boiling water, stirring until smooth, then cool to room temperature.

3. Use a small cup and dissolve the instant coffee in the boiling water and set aside for later.

4. Use a small bowl and mix together the baking powder, salt, and flour, then set aside for later.

5. Use a large bowl to mix together the butter, white sugar, brown sugar, and coffee, beating until the mixture becomes creamy.

6. Mix in the egg and the melted chocolate chips and then gradually add the flour mixture. When mixed, add the rest of the chocolate chips and the chopped walnuts.

7. Using ungreased cookie sheets, or baking trays, drop a tablespoon of the mixture for each cookie, flattening to about 3 inches (8cm) each.

8. Bake in the oven for 10 to 12 minutes until done.

9. Allow to stand for approximately 5 minutes before removing from the baking sheets or trays and then cool completely on a wire rack.

11. Crumbly Butter Cookies

Make 4 to 5 dozen cookies

1 cup butter

1 cup sugar

1 tbsp milk

1 egg

1 tsp vanilla essence

2¾ cups plain flour

¼ tsp salt

1 tsp baking powder

1. Preheat the oven to 350 degrees F, 180 degrees C or Gas Mark 4.

2. Use a large bowl and mix together the butter and sugar until creamy and light. Add the milk, egg, and vanilla essence, until smooth.

3. Use a medium bowl and mix together the flour, salt, and baking powder.

4. Gradually mix in the flour mixture to the butter and egg mixture to get a dough consistency.

5. Lightly flour a flat even surface and roll out the dough to a thickness of 1/8th inch (3mm).

6. Cut the dough into desired shapes and place on a cookie sheet or baking tray.

7. Place in the oven for 8 to 10 minutes until light brown, then remove and place on wire racks to cool.

12. Ginger Cookies

Makes approx 48 cookies

¾ cup butter

1 cup sugar

1 egg

¼ cup molasses

2½ cups plain flour

1 tsp ground cinnamon

1 tsp ground ginger

1 tsp ground cloves

1½ tsp baking powder

Powdered sugar

1. Preheat the oven to 350 degrees F, 180 degrees C or Gas Mark 4.

2. Use a medium bowl and mix together the butter and sugar until a creamy mixture.

3. Add the egg and molasses and thoroughly mix, then add the flour, ground cinnamon, ground ginger, ground cloves, and baking powder, until dough is formed.

4. Roll dough into golf ball sized balls and roll in the powdered sugar.

5. Place on an ungreased baking sheet or tray and flatten slightly.

6. Bake for 5 to 7 minutes until just beginning to turn brown.

7. Let cool for 1 minute then remove to wire racks to cool completely.

13. Butterscotch Fudge

Makes 64 pieces

1 tsp butter

2/3rd cup evaporated milk

2 tbsp butter

1+2/3rd cups sugar

½ tsp salt

2 cups miniature marshmallows

1 x 10 oz (285g) packet butterscotch chips

½ cup chopped walnuts

1 tsp maple flavoring

1. Line an 8 inch (20cm) square with foil and grease the foil with the 1 tsp butter in preparation.

2. Use a large saucepan to mix together the evaporated milk, butter, sugar, and salt, and boil for 5 minutes, stirring continuously.

3. Remove from the heat and add the marshmallows, butterscotch chips, chopped walnuts, and maple flavoring. Continue stirring until all the chips and marshmallows have melted.

4. When chips and marshmallows have melted, pour the mixture into the prepared pan and allow to set.

5. When set, lift the fudge from the pan using the foil. Discard the foil and cut into 1 inch (25mm) squares.

6. Store in an airtight container until ready to serve.

14. Turkey Stuffing

Serves 5

1 white loaf (fresh or stale)

1 medium onion, finely chopped

1 tsp savory seasoning

Pinch of salt

Pinch ground black pepper

1. Use a medium bowl and moisten the bread with just enough water to make it moist.

2. Add the chopped onion, savory seasoning, salt, and pepper, and mix together with your hands.

3. Place the mixture in a pie tin, and cover with foil.

4. Bake with the turkey for at least an hour (1½ hours works well). Remove the foil for the last 15 minutes to make it slightly crunchy.

15. Fruity Brown Rice Stuffing

Serves 6

1 chopped medium onion

8 tbsp butter

2 cups brown rice

4 cups water

½ cup chopped fresh parsley

1 tsp crumbled leaf sage

2 cups halved pecans

2 cups chopped dried apricots

1 cup chopped apples

1 cup raisins

2 cups chopped celery

1 tsp salt

1. Use a large saucepan to sauté (brown quickly) the onion in the butter until soft. This should take about 5 minutes.

2. Add the rice and water and bring to the boil. When boiling, lower the heat, cover and simmer until the rice has absorbed all the water.

3. Remove the saucepan from the heat and stir in the parsley, sage, pecans, apricots, apple, raisins, celery and salt until thoroughly mixed.

4. Apportion and serve.

16. Sausage & Sage Stuffing

Serves 6 to 8

2 loaves white bread diced into ½ inch (1cm) cubes

1 lb (455g) sausage meat

2 chicken bouillon cubes

3 eggs

2 stems chopped celery

1 chopped onion

¼ cup grated Parmesan cheese

1 tbsp chopped fresh parsley

1 tsp sage

Salt & pepper to taste

1. Use a large bowl and place the bread cubes in it.

2. Use a skillet or frying pan and fry the sausage meat until browned. Drain off the excess fat.

3. Dissolve the chicken bouillon cubes in 2 cups of water.

4. Add all the ingredients to the large bowl with the bread cubes and mix everything together well.

5. Stuff the bird with the mixture or put the mixture into a separate baking tin.

6. Bake in the oven for 1 hour at 250 degrees F, 180 degrees C or Gas Mark 4.

17. Garlic Potatoes

Serves 2

1 lb (455g) small clean new potatoes

6 crushed cloves garlic

2 tbsp olive oil

½ tsp salt

Ground pepper to taste

1. Place all the ingredients in a microwave-proof casserole dish and stir a couple of time to mix the ingredients and coat the potatoes.

2. Cover the dish and place in the microwave on high for 10 to 15 minutes, stirring every 5 minutes.

3. Check the potatoes are done, and cook further if not.

4. When done, portion and serve.

18. Yam Soufflé

Serves 4 to 6

1 cup milk

3 tbsp butter

½ cup sugar

2 cups mashed yam

1 tsp ground nutmeg

½ tsp salt

2 separated eggs

½ cup chopped pecans

½ cup raisins

1. Preheat the oven to 350 degrees F, 180 degrees C or Gas Mark 4.

2. Lightly grease a baking dish in preparation.

3. Use a medium saucepan and boil the milk.

4. Use a medium bowl and mix together the boiled milk, butter, sugar, mashed yam, ground nutmeg, and salt.

5. Use a small bowl to beat the egg yolks then add to the yam mixture with the chopped pecans and raisins.

6. Use a small bowl to beat the egg whites until stiffened and fold into the yam mixture.

7. Pour the complete mixture into the prepared baking tin.

8. Place in the oven for 50 minutes to 1 hour, until it becomes firm.

19. Apple & Raisin Stuffing

Serves up to 8

¾ cup finely chopped onion

1½ cups chopped celery

1 cup butter

7 cups bread cubes

1 tsp thyme

1½ tsp crushed sage leaf

¾ cup raisins

3 cups finely chopped apples

1 tsp salt

½ tsp pepper

1. Use a large skillet or frying pan and fry the onion and celery in the butter until the onion is cooked.

2. Stir in 2 cups of the bread cubes and then pour into a large bowl.

3. Add the thyme, sage, raisins, apples, the rest of the bread cubes, salt, and pepper, and thoroughly stir.

4. Stuff the bird and roast.

20. Eggplant (Aubergine) Salad

Serves 8

2 eggplants

2 tbsp olive oil

1 thinly sliced cucumber

1 thinly sliced onion

½ cup cider vinegar

2 tbsp brown sugar

½ tsp salt

1. Cut the ends of the eggplants and cut into ½ inch (1cm) slices.

2. Brush the eggplants slices with olive oil and grill until brown and soft, turning regularly. This should take 15 to 20 minutes.

3. Use a small bowl and lay the cucumber and onion slices in enough iced water to cover. Lightly squash the cucumber and onion slices to barely bruise them and bring out the flavor. Cover the bowl and chill in the refrigerator for 30 minutes.

4. Use a medium bowl to mix together the cider vinegar, sugar, and salt. Add the cucumber and onion slices.

5. Roughly chop the eggplant and put into a serving bowl or plate.

6. Top with the cucumber and onion mixture and serve.

21. Glazed Yams

Serves 8

½ cup butter

2 lb (910g) cooked yams

¼ cup maple syrup

1. Preheat the oven to 350 degrees F, 180 degrees C or Gas Mark 4.

2. Put the butter into a baking dish and melt in the oven as it preheats, remove from oven when the butter has melted.

3. Leave the yams whole if they are small, or cut into 2 inch (25mm) chunks if they are large.

4. Put the yams into the melted butter and turn to coat all over.

5. Carefully pour the maple syrup over the yams to evenly cover.

6. Bake in the oven for 25 to 30 minutes until thoroughly heated through.

7. Pour into a serving dish and serve hot.

22. Saucy Cauliflower

Serves 6 to 10

1 cauliflower

¼ cup chopped green pepper

4 oz (115g) sliced mushrooms

¼ cup butter

1/3rd cup plain flour

2 cups milk

1 cup grated cheese

2 tbsp chopped pimento

1 tsp salt

1. Preheat the oven to 325 degrees F, 170 degrees C or Gas Mark 3.

2. Lightly grease a casserole dish in preparation.

3. Break the cauliflower into separate florets and boil in hot water in a saucepan until tender-crisp. This should take 8 to 10 minutes, then drain.

4. Use a medium saucepan to sauté the green pepper and mushrooms in butter until tender.

5. Add the flour and mix thoroughly and then add the milk and stir to mix thoroughly.

6. Cook whilst stirring until you have a smooth thick and creamy mixture then add the grated cheese, chopped pimento, and salt, and mix thoroughly.

7. Place half the cauliflower florets into the casserole dish and pour half the sauce over. Add the remaining cauliflower florets then cover with the remaining sauce.

8. Bake for about 15 minutes, until bubbling.

9. Serve hot.

23. Honey Glazed Ham

Serves 8 to 10

1 cooked ham – about 10 to 12 lbs (approx 5 kg)

1 x 10 oz (285g) packet of frozen chopped kale cabbage

½ cup finely chopped celery tops

1 cup finely chopped spinach

1 cup finely chopped onion

¼ tsp pepper

1 tsp salt

2 tbsp cider vinegar

2 tsp dry mustard

½ cup honey

1. Preheat the oven to 325 degrees F, 170 degrees C or Gas Mark 3.

2. If there is any rind on the ham, trim off to within ¼ inch (5mm) of the meat.

3. Make small cross cuts in the fatty side of the ham with a small vegetable knife approx 2 inch (50mm) deep and about 1 inch (25mm) apart.

4. Place the frozen kale in a large saucepan with enough boiling, salted water to cover, following any instruction on the packet.

5. When thawed, drain, and then squeeze out any excess water.

6. Use a medium bowl and mix together the kale, chopped celery tops, chopped spinach, chopped onion, pepper, and salt.

7. Press this mixture into the crosses you have made in the ham fat.

8. Place the ham into a shallow roasting tin, fat side up and place in the oven to bake for 5 minutes, to start to warm it through.

9. Mix together the cider vinegar, dry mustard, and honey, and brush over the ham.

10. Roast the ham for a further 30 minutes, basting regularly with the honey glaze mixture.

11. Allow to rest for 20 minutes before carving.

12. Carefully hold the ham together when carving to keep the stuffing in place.

24. Roast Turkey

Serves 8

12 lb (5.5Kg) whole turkey

6 tbsp butter

4 cups water

3 tbsp chicken broth

2 tbsp dried chopped parsley

2 tbsp dried chopped onion

Salt to season

1. Preheat oven to 350 degrees F, 180 degrees C, or Gas Mark 4.

2. Wash the turkey inside and out and pat dry with paper towels. Discard the giblets unless anyone wishes to eat them or you wish to use them for stock or gravy. (they make a wonderful stock. See Recipe 32)

3. Pull the skin from the breast gently so that it separates from the meat without removing it and spread the butter evenly between the breasts on either side between the skin and the meat. Put the skin back into place. Don't worry if it is a little saggy. It will tighten again during cooking.

4. Use a medium bowl and mix together the water and the chicken broth. Add the parsley and onion and thoroughly mix.

5. Place the turkey, breast side up in a large roasting tin, pour the broth mixture over the top of the turkey, sprinkle salt to season and cover loosely with foil.

6. Place in the oven for 4 to 5 hours until done and the juices run clear when pierced. For the last 30 to 45 minutes of cooking, remove the foil to allow the turkey skin to brown and crisp up slightly.

7. Stuffing of your choice can be cooked inside the bird and included at the start of preparations, or cooked separately in a roasting tin.

25. Turkey left-over's Casserole

Serves 4

4 oz (115g) noodles

1 pack frozen broccoli

2 tbsp butter

2 tbsp plain flour

2 cups milk

¼ tsp ready mustard

1 tsp salt

¼ tsp pepper

1 cup grated cheese

2 cups chopped cooked turkey

1. Preheat the oven to 350 degrees F, 180 degrees C or Gas Mark 4.

2. Use a medium saucepan and boil the noodles in water until ready. This will take about 10 minutes.

3. Use a medium saucepan and boil the broccoli in water until cooked. This will also take about 10 minutes.

4. Use a medium saucepan and over a low heat add the butter and melt it. Add the flour, milk, mustard, salt, and pepper, and thoroughly mix, stirring whilst it comes to the boil until thickened.

5. Remove from the heat and stir in the cheese until it is melted.

6. Drain the noodles and broccoli. Chop the stems of the broccoli, but leave the florets intact.

7. Use a medium casserole dish and arrange the chopped broccoli stems, noodles, and turkey, around the bottom of the dish.

8. Pour the cheese sauce over the other ingredients and then lightly press the broccoli florets into the top of the sauce.

9. Place in the oven and bake uncovered for 15 minutes, until bubbling.

26. Turkey Left-over's Hash

Serves 4

<u>Hash</u>

2 tbsp butter

1 thinly sliced onion

½ cup chopped celery

3 cups chopped cooked turkey (or Chicken)

<u>Sauce</u>

2 tbsp butter

3 tbsp plain flour

2½ cups water

½ tsp salt

½ tsp pepper

¼ cup cream

<u>Biscuits</u>

2 cups plain flour

1 tsp salt

1 tbsp baking powder

2 beaten eggs

¾ cup cream

<u>Hash</u>

1. Use a skillet or frying pan and over a low heat melt the butter. Add the onion slices and chopped celery and stir for 5 to 8 minutes. Add the chopped turkey pieces and cook for a further 5 minutes.

Sauce

2. Use a medium saucepan and heat the butter until bubbling, and mix in the flour, then add the water, salt, and pepper, and mix thoroughly.

3. When the mixture is smooth and creamy add the cream and mix in. Pour over the turkey hash and simmer for 15 minutes.

Biscuits

4. Use a medium bowl and mix together the flour, salt, and baking powder.

5. Use a small bowl to mix together the eggs and cream. When thoroughly blended, add to the flour mixture and mix in just enough to moisten the flour. Try to gain a consistency of soft and lumpy dough by not stirring too much.

6. Drop the mixture in tablespoonfuls onto a greased baking sheet or baking tray and cook for about 15 minutes at 400 degrees F, 200 degrees C or Gas Mark 6 until golden brown.

7. Portion the hash and serve hot with hot biscuits.

27. Ham with White Wine Sauce

Serves 10

1 tbsp butter

¾ cup thinly sliced carrots

¾ cup chopped onion

1 boneless cooked ham - 5 to 6 lb (2.3 to 2.7 Kg)

6 crushed peppercorns

2 bay leaves

¼ tsp powdered cloves

6 sprigs parsley

½ tsp dried thyme

4 cups white wine

3 tbsp mustard

¼ cup apple jelly

2 cups chicken stock

10½ tbsp cold water

10½ tbsp cornstarch

1. Preheat the oven to 350 degrees F, 180 degrees C or Gas Mark 4.

2. Use a large roasting pan over a medium heat to melt the butter. When the butter is melted, sauté the carrots and onions until softened. This will take about 3 minutes.

3. Place the ham joint, fat side up, on top of the vegetables. Add the peppercorns, bay leaves, cloves, parsley, thyme, and 3 cups of white wine, to the pan and bring to a simmer. Remove from the heat and cover.

4. Transfer the roasting tin to the oven and roast for approximately 1½ hours until done and the meat is tender when pierced with a knife. Baste the meat about every 20 minutes with the juices from the roasting tin.

5. Remove the roasting tin from the oven and raise the temperature to 450 degrees F, 230 degrees C or Gas Mark 8.

6. Use a small saucepan over a low heat and mix together the mustard and jelly, until the jelly is dissolved.

7. Brush the mixture over the surface of the ham and return the roasting tin to the oven and cook for a further 15 minutes – uncovered.

8. Remove the tin from the oven. Remove the ham onto a serving platter and cover loosely with aluminum foil. Allow to rest for 20 minutes whilst making the sauce.

9. Remove and discard the parsley and bay leaves from the roasting tin and place the remaining ingredients from the tin into a blender and puree.

10. Pour the pureed vegetables back into the roasting tin and place the tin back on the cooker top over a high heat. Add the stock and remaining 1 cup of white wine and stir until the sauce is reduced by about a quarter.

11. In a medium bowl, mix together the water and cornstarch to make a smooth paste.

12. Add the cornstarch paste to the sauce and continue to cook whilst whisking together until the ingredients thicken a little.

13. To serve: slice the ham and arrange on a serving plate with the sauce poured over.

28. Holiday Ham with Mustard Sauce

Serves 8

Ham

1 cooked ham about 5 lb (2.3Kg)

2 tbsp brandy

½ tsp ground cloves

1 cup brown sugar

¼ tsp ground cinnamon

¼ tsp ground ginger

2 tbsp plain flour

Mustard Sauce

½ cup sour cream

½ cup mayonnaise

3 tbsp mustard

Ham

1. Preheat the oven to 325 degrees F, 170 degrees C or Gas Mark 3.

2. Place the ham, fat side up, in a roasting tin and cook until the ham is until brown and tender, which should be about half an hour longer than the packaging call for.

3. Using a small bowl mix together the brandy, cloves, brown sugar, cinnamon, ginger, and flour, to make a paste.

4. Remove the ham from the oven and turn the oven up to 425 degrees F, 220 degrees C or Gas Mark 7.

5. Remove the skin from the ham with a sharp knife, leaving about ½ inch (1cm) of fat, then score the surface of the ham with the knife using diagonal cuts to leave a diamond pattern.

6. Rub the paste over the surface of the ham and return to the oven for a further 20 minutes while you make the mustard sauce.

Mustard Sauce
7. Use a medium saucepan over a medium heat, whisk together the sour cream and mayonnaise.

8. Blend in the mustard and heat through until almost boiled.

Serve in a sauce boat.

29. Beef Eye Roast

Serves 12

3 lb (1.4 Kg) lean beef rib eye joint

½ cup red wine vinegar

¼ cup water

3 tbsp olive oil

3 crushed cloves garlic

1 tbsp fresh thyme

½ tsp crushed red pepper

1. Cut the roast down the middle, and lay it open and flat in a baking dish.

2. Use a small bowl to mix together the red wine vinegar, water, olive oil, garlic, thyme, and red pepper. Pour the mixture over the roast and cover.

3. Allow the meat to marinate for at least 12 hours, turning occasionally.

4. Remove the meat and place on a rack in a broiling pan. Discard the marinade.

5. Broil the meat about 6 inches (15cm) from the heat, for approximately 25 minutes, turning occasionally until the required cooked finish is achieved.

6. Remove from the heat and cover with aluminum foil for 15 minutes before carving.

7. Pour the remaining juices over the sliced meat before serving.

30. Roast Goose with Stuffing

Serves 8

1 peeled and chopped apple

10 quartered dried figs

2½ cups crumbled corn bread

3 tbsp chopped fresh parsley

2 tsp chopped fresh savory

Salt & pepper to taste

1 Goose - approx 9 to 12 lb (4 to 5.5Kg)

2 tbsp plain flour

1 ½ cups reserved goose broth

1. Preheat the oven to 325 degrees F, 170 degrees C, or Gas Mark 3.

2. Use a small saucepan and place the neck and gizzard in 2 pints (1.14Lt) water and slowly bring to the boil, then simmer, partially covered, for a couple of hours until there is about 2 cups of stock remaining.

3. Use a medium bowl and mix together the chopped apple, figs, corn bread, parsley and savory. Add salt and pepper to taste and stuff the goose.

4. Place the goose in a large roasting tin, breast down, place in the oven and roast for 1½ hours, drawing the fat off as it cooks. A goose will produce a lot of fat so be prepared to take off quite a lot.

5. Turn the goose over, and place back in the oven to cook for a further 1½ hours until done, and the juices run clear when pierced.

6. Place the goose on a serving platter and allow it to rest whilst you make the gravy.

7. Use the roasting tin over a low heat and add 2 tablespoons of the goose fat. Sprinkle with the flour and stir, using all the remaining juices in the pan. Add the goose broth from earlier and stir until smooth. Add salt and pepper to taste and pour into a gravy boat for presentation.

31. Cranberry Glazed Roast Pork

Serves 11

2 x 16 oz (455g) cans jellied cranberry sauce

½ cup cranberry juice

¼ tsp ground cloves

1 tsp powdered mustard

½ cup sugar

4 lb (1.8 Kg) Pork Roast

2 tbsp cornstarch

2 tbsp cold water

Salt to season

1. Preheat the oven to 275 degrees F, 140 degrees C or Gas Mark 1.

2. Use a small bowl to mash the cranberry sauce, stirring in the cranberry juice, cloves, mustard, and sugar.

3. Place the pork in a large roasting tin and pour the cranberry mixture over the meat.

4. Place in the oven and roast for 6 to 8 hours, until the meat is tender.

5. Skim the fat from the juices in the roasting tin, then pour 2 cups of the remaining liquid into a small saucepan.

6. Blend together the cornstarch and water in a small bowl and when smooth add to the saucepan and stir together over a medium heat. Bring to a boil and simmer gently, stirring continuously until the mixture thickens.

7. Season with salt and serve with the roast.

32. Meatballs, Swedish Style

Serves 4 to 8

2 cups soft bread crumbs

2/3rd cup milk

4 tbsp butter

½ cup finely chopped onion

1½ lb (680g) ground (minced) beef

1 tsp paprika

1 tsp ground nutmeg

3 lightly beaten eggs

2 tsp salt

½ tsp pepper

1 tbsp concentrated meat extract

3 tbsp plain flour

1 cup water

1 cup sour cream

2 tbsp finely chopped fresh parsley

1. Use a medium bowl and soak the breadcrumbs in milk until softened.

2. Use a small saucepan over a low heat to melt 1 tbsp of the butter and then cook the onion.

3. Add the onions to the softened breadcrumbs, then mix in the meat. Add the paprika, nutmeg, eggs, salt, and pepper, and thoroughly mix.

4. Shape the mixture into small balls.

5. Use a skillet or frying pan and heat the remaining 3 tbsp of butter over a medium heat and fry the meatballs until a golden brown.

6. Remove the meatballs and add the meat extract and 3 tbsp of flour, stirring until thoroughly mixed. Add water and continue to stir and cook until thickened.

7. Reduce the heat to low and cook for a further 5 minutes whilst stirring. Gradually add the sour cream, a little at a time and stir in.

8. Add the meatballs and simmer, covered for approximately 10 minutes, sprinkle with a garnish of parsley and it is ready to serve.

33. Roast Turkey with Cornbread Stuffing

Serves 10

4 oz (115g) Butter

1 fresh turkey – 12 to 16 lb (5.5 to 7.3 Kg)

8 oz (225g) thinly sliced salt pork

Stuffing

Corn Bread Stuffing

2 packets corn bread mix

½ cup chopped celery

1 finely chopped onion

½ cup butter

2 egg yolks

Salt & pepper to taste

Turkey Stock

Turkey giblets, neck & wing tips

3 cups water

½ sliced onion

1/8th tsp chopped rosemary

1/8th tsp chopped thyme

1/8th tsp chopped basil

½ bay leaf

½ crushed clove of garlic

Pinch of salt

Turkey Giblet Gravy

¼ cup pan drippings

¼ cup flour

1 cup water

2 cups turkey stock

Turkey giblets, cooked and chopped

Salt & pepper to taste

Turkey

1. Preheat the oven to 425 degrees F, 220 degrees C, or Gas Mark 7.

2. Cut the butter into thin slices and place in the freezer whilst you ready the turkey.

3. Wash the turkey thoroughly, removing the giblets, neck and wing tips, reserving for later, and pat dry with paper toweling.

4. Begin at the breast and loosen the skin from the meat by gradually working your fingers between them as far as you can go. Do not remove the skin, but leave it free. Work your way down the legs about half-way.

5. Use the slices of butter and place them between the skin and the meat, pressing the skin back into place afterwards. It may be a little baggy, but it will soon tighten once it is in the oven. Loosely wrap the turkey in foil and refrigerate whilst you prepare the stuffing.

65

6. Stuff the turkey at the neck end. You can also stuff at the bottom end if you wish or place any leftover stuffing in a small baking dish and place in the oven about 30 minutes before the turkey is finished cooking.

7. Place the turkey on a rack in a large roasting tin on its' side and cover the breast with strips of salt pork, holding them in place with cocktail sticks. Place in the oven and cook for 15 minutes, then turn the turkey on to its' other side and cook for another 15 minutes.

8. Lower the oven temperature to 325 degrees F, 170 degrees C, or Gas Mark 3 and continue roasting the turkey, turning regularly and basting with the juices in the pan for 3½ to 4 hours until done and the juices run clear. For the last 15 minutes of roasting time, turn the turkey breast side up and remove the pork strips and discard.

9 Remove the turkey to a serving plate when done and allow to rest for 30 minutes before carving.

Stuffing

10. Prepare the corn bread following the instructions on the packet. Allow to cool then crumble the bread and pour 7 cups of the bread crumbs into a medium bowl.

11. Use a skillet or frying pan over a medium heat and sauté the celery and onion in butter until soft. Pour the contents of the skillet or frying pan over the bread crumbs in the bowl.

12. In a medium bowl, whisk the eggs and then add the stock and mix together. Add to the bread crumb mixture and stir gently to mix together. Add salt and pepper to season according to your own taste. Go to #6.

Turkey Stock

13. Use a large saucepan put in the water and place in it the giblets, neck and wing tips, and add the onion, rosemary, thyme, basil, bay leaf, garlic, and salt. Bring to the boil then lower the heat and simmer for about 15 minutes until the liver is tender. Remove the liver and set aside. Continue to simmer the mixture for a further hour, or until the giblets are tender. Remove from the heat and strain the liquid, reserving the stock and finely chopping the giblets for the gravy.

Turkey Giblet Gravy

14. Pour all the fat from the roasting tin into a measuring jug and from the jug measure ¼ cup and return to the roasting tin over a low heat on the cooker top. Sprinkle the flour over the turkey fat and stir for 2 or 3 minutes. Add the water and 2 cups of the turkey stock and continue to stir from all round the pan for a further 2 minutes until the gravy thickens and bubbles.

15. Strain the gravy and add the chopped turkey giblets, seasoning as necessary.

34. Roast Leg of Lamb

Serves 8

5 lb (2.25 kg) leg of lamb

4 slices garlic cloves

Salt & ground black pepper to taste

2 tbsp fresh rosemary

1. Preheat the oven to 350 degrees F, 180 degrees C or Gas Mark 4.

2. Cut slits along the top of the leg just deep enough to push the slices of garlic into the meat.

3. Shake salt and pepper all over the joint.

4. Place several sprigs of rosemary in the bottom of the roasting tin and the remainder on top of the lamb.

5 Place in the oven and cook until done. This should take about 2 hours, but take care not to overcook. The flavor always seems to be best when the meat is still slightly pink.

35. Seasonal Rice Pudding

Serves 4

6 oz (170g) rice

1½ oz (40g) sugar

1 pint (570ml) milk

2 cups water

14½ oz (400g) evaporated milk

3 eggs

¼ tsp ground nutmeg

1 tsp vanilla extract

1 oz (28g) butter

1 tsp salt

½ tsp ground cinnamon

1. Preheat the oven to 350 degrees F, 180 degrees C or Gas Mark 4.

2. Use a large casserole dish and put the rice and sugar into the bottom, giving a little stir.

3. Use a medium bowl and add the milk, water, evaporated milk, eggs, nutmeg, and vanilla extract.

4. Whisk the mixture and add the butter and salt, giving a further whisk.

5. Pour the mixture over the rice in the casserole dish, give a stir and sprinkle cinnamon over the top.

6. Place the casserole in a pan of water, put it in the oven and cook for 1 hour, or until it sets.

36. Cooling Christmas Fruit Salad

Serves 6

3 peeled oranges

3 peeled and chopped apples

1 small can crushed pineapple

1 cup chopped pecans

1 cup miniature marshmallows

2 tsp Mayonnaise

2 tsp sugar

1. This is nice and simple. Using a large bowl mix all the ingredients thoroughly and refrigerate.

Serve chilled

37. Christmas Pudding

Serves 8 to 10

1 small cooking apple (peeled, cored and finely chopped with juice)

1lb (455g) dried mixed fruit (raisins, sultanas & currants)

1 oz (28g) chopped mixed candied peel

4 tbsp brandy

½ lemon

½ orange

2 oz (55g) self-raising flour

1½ tsp ground cinnamon

1 tsp ground mixed spice

4oz (115g) brown sugar

Zest from ½ a lemon

Zest from ½ an orange

4 oz (115g) white fresh bread crumbs

4 oz (115g) shredded suet

1 oz (28g) chopped almonds

2 eggs

1. Lightly grease a 2 ½ pint (1.4 ltr) pudding bowl.

2. Use a large bowl and mix together the apple, dried fruits, candied peel, brandy, squeeze the juice from the half lemon, and the half orange, and thoroughly mix into the mixture. Cover with a tea towel and leave to marinate overnight.

3. Use another large bowl to mix together the flour, cinnamon, and mixed spice. Add the brown sugar, zest from the half lemon, and the half orange, bread crumbs, suet, and almonds, and thoroughly mix together.

4. When mixed add the marinated fruits and thoroughly mix these together.

5. Use a small bowl and beat the eggs. Add the beaten eggs to the dry mixture and mix again. This should produce a soft mixture.

6. Spoon the mixture into the greased pudding bowl, pressing the mixture in well with the spoon.

7. Cover with a double layer of greaseproof or parchment paper and then a layer of aluminum foil and secure with string.

8. Place the pudding in a steamer, over a saucepan of simmering water, and steam the pudding for 7 hours. Keep topping the water up in the saucepan as necessary. When done, the pudding should be a dark brown color and heavy.

9. Take the pudding from the steamer and allow it to cool completely. Remove the paper and stab a skewer

into it a few times. Pour a little more brandy over the top and cover again with more greaseproof paper and tie off with string. Store in a cool dry place until Christmas.

10. On Christmas day, reheat the pudding by steaming for about an hour.

Notes:

A tradition when making the Christmas pudding is for every member of the family to have a turn at mixing. When you get to #5 in the instructions is a good time for each to have a stir and at the same time make a wish.

Christmas pudding is not meant to be eaten immediately and is traditionally made in Britain from September until the end of November. The pudding would be likely to collapse if eaten immediately and the flavors would not have had time to mature throughout the whole pudding.

Why not make a few puddings earlier than this and then you will have time to "test" the recipe?

38. Christmas Pudding Sauce

Serves 6

2 tbsp cornstarch

½ cup sugar

1 beaten egg

1 cup hot water

Pinch of salt

2 tbsp butter

1. Use a medium saucepan to mix together the cornstarch and sugar. Add the beaten egg, hot water and salt and stir over a medium heat until thickened.

2. Add the butter and stir until melted and mixed in.

3. Pour over the Christmas pudding.

39. Caramel Flan

Serves 6

½ cup sugar

6 eggs

2 cans sweetened condensed milk

2 cans water (use empty cans above)

1 tsp vanilla extract

Pinch of salt

1. Preheat the oven to 350 degrees F, 180 degrees C or Gas Mark 4.

2. Place a large shallow pan of water inside the oven

3. Use a sturdy saucepan and over a medium heat add the sugar with a few drops of water.

4. Constantly stir until the sugar caramelizes and then pour quickly into a one-piece tube pan.

5. Use a large bowl to beat the eggs, then add the milk, the water, vanilla extract, and salt, and mix thoroughly.

6. Pour the mixture over the caramel in the tube pan and cover with foil.

7. Carefully place in the pan of water in the oven and bake for about 40 minutes until a knife will come out clean when inserted. You may need to keep checking

every few minutes after about 25 minutes to see if it is done in order to avoid over-cooking.

8. Loosen the edges and turn out onto a plate.

40. Derby Pie

Serves 6

1 cup sugar

½ cup + 2 tbsp plain flour

2 beaten eggs

½ cup melted & cooled butter

1 cup chopped pecans

1 tsp vanilla extract

1 cup chocolate chips

1 unbaked pie shell

1. Preheat the oven to 350 degrees F, 180 degrees C or Gas Mark 4.

2. Use a medium bowl to mix together the sugar and flour. Add the eggs and mix in, then add the butter.

3. Add the pecans, vanilla extract, and chocolate, and mix together, then pour into the pie crust.

4. Bake in the oven for 30 minutes until done. The pie should be chewy and slightly soft in the center but not runny.

41. Raspberry Topsy-Turvy Cake

Serves 6

2 cups raspberries (fresh or frozen)

1 small box of lemon custard

1 egg

1¾ cups plain flour

¾ cup sugar

¼ cup shortening

2 tsp baking powder

1 tsp grated lemon zest

1. Preheat the oven to 350 degrees F, 180 degrees C or Gas Mark 4.

2. Layer the raspberries over the bottom of a 8 inch (20cm) x 8 inch (20cm) baking dish.

3. Spread the lemon custard over the raspberries.

4. Use a medium bowl and mix together the egg, flour, sugar, shortening, baking powder, and lemon zest, to a smooth mix, and spread over the lemon custard.

5. Bake in the oven for 45 minutes until done and turn out onto a plate with the raspberries at the top.

42. Chocolate Log

Serves 10

Cake

¾ cup plain flour

½ tsp baking powder

½ tsp salt

5 eggs

¾ cup sugar

2½ cups chocolate

¼ cup cold water

2 tbsp sugar

1 cup confectioners sugar

Frosting

1 packet Dream Whip

½ tsp mint flavoring

½ cup milk

Cake

1. Preheat the oven to 350 degrees F, 180 degrees C or Gas Mark 4.

2. Line a 15 inch (38cm) x 10 inch (25cm) jelly roll pan with greased wax paper in preparation.

3. Use a medium bowl to mix together the flour, baking powder and salt.

4. Beat the eggs and then add to the flour and gently mix together.

5. Gradually beat in the ¾ cup of sugar.

6. Use another medium bowl and melt the chocolate. Add the water, and the 2 tbsp sugar until a smooth mixture is reached. Add to the batter and mix thoroughly together.

7. Pour the mixture into the lined jelly roll pan and bake in the oven for approximately 20 minutes until cooked.

8. Sprinkle a clean tea towel with confectioners' sugar and turn the cake out onto the towel.

9. Remove the paper, trim the edges and roll in the towel. Leave for 30 minutes to cool.

Frosting

10. Beat the Dream whip with the mint flavoring and milk until stiff peaks form.

11. Unroll the cake and discard the towel. Spread the dream whip over the cake and chill until ready to serve.

43. Traditional Christmas Cake

Serves 12

2/3rd cup butter

1 cup brown sugar

4 eggs

2 cups plain flour

2 tbsp chopped crystallized ginger

1 tsp allspice

1tsp ground cinnamon

¼ tsp ground cloves

1 small box glace peel

1 small box glace cherries

1 cup raisins

1 cup currants

½ cup chopped walnuts

1. Preheat the oven to 325 degrees F, 170 degrees C or Gas Mark 3.

2. Lightly grease and flour a 3 inch (8cm) deep, circular baking tin in preparation.

3. Use a large bowl and cream together the butter and sugar. Add the eggs and beat into the mixture.

4. Add about half of the flour with the ginger, allspice, ground cinnamon and ground cloves and thoroughly mix.

5. Dust the fruit and nuts with some flour and mix in with the rest of the flour. The mixture will be stiff.

6. Spoon the mixture into the prepared tin and bake in the oven for 2 hours.

7. Check to see if the cake is cooked throughout by testing with a fine skewer. Insert it into the centre of the cake; if it comes out clean, it is cooked. If it shows any batter, bake for up to a further 30 minutes. If the top of the cake is already dark and it needs more cooking, cover lightly with foil.

44. German Christmas Cake

Serves 12

1lb (455g) raisins

1 cup hot water

1lb (455g) pork sausage meat

1 tsp baking powder

1lb (455g) brown sugar

1lb (455g) halved walnuts

1lb (455g) pitted dates

2½ cups plain flour

1 cup mixed candied fruits

1 tsp ground cinnamon

1 tsp ground cloves

½ tsp ground allspice

Pinch of salt

1. Preheat the oven to 375 degrees F, 190 degrees C or Gas Mark 5.

2. Lightly grease 6 or 7 small loaf tins 5 inches (13cm) x 3 inches (8cm) in preparation.

3. Put the raisins into a medium bowl and add the hot water. The raisins will gradually plump up.

4. Use a large bowl and place the sausage meat into it. Sprinkle with baking powder and add the water that the raisins were in. Use your hands to mix together gently.

5. Gradually add the remaining ingredients one by one, mixing together as you go.

6. Spoon the mixture into the prepared small loaf tins and bake in the oven for 2½ hours.

Note: It is advisable to make the cakes about a month ahead of when required for best results.

Store in a cool, dry and dark place.

45. Danish Christmas Cake

Serves 12

<u>Cake</u>

3 cups plain flour

1 lb (455g) chopped dates

2 cups chopped pecans

1 small bottle of maraschino cherries with juice

1 ¾ cups sugar

1 cup margarine

3 eggs

1½ tsp baking powder

1 tsp salt

1 cup buttermilk

1 tsp vanilla extract

1 tbsp grated orange zest

1 tbsp orange juice

<u>Sauce</u>

1 cup orange juice

1 cup shredded coconut

½ cup sugar

<u>Cake</u>

1. Preheat the oven to 350 degrees F, 180 degrees C or Gas Mark 4.

2. Grease a large circular cake tin in preparation.

3. Lightly flour the dates, nuts, and cherries. (This prevents them from dropping to the bottom of the pan)

4. Use a large bowl and cream together the sugar and margarine. Add the eggs to the mixture one at a time.

5. Add the flour, baking powder and salt and thoroughly mix together.

6. Add the buttermilk, and vanilla extract, and mix.

7. Add the floured dates, pecans, and cherries, mixing thoroughly.

8. Add the orange zest and orange juice and give the mixture a thorough mixing together.

9. Pour the batter into the prepared cake tin and bake in the oven for one hour until the cake tests show it is done.

Sauce

10. Whilst the cake is cooking, mix together the orange juice, shredded coconut, and sugar, in a small bowl.

11. Pour the sauce over the hot cake to serve.

46. Dark Christmas Cake

Serves 12

1 cup halved candied cherries

½ cup chopped preserved lemon peel

½ cup chopped preserved orange peel

3 cups raisins

1 cup halved almonds

1 cup halved pecans

1 cup currants

1½ cups chopped preserved citron

1 cup chopped preserved pineapple

2 cups plain flour

1½ tsp ground cinnamon

1½ tsp ground cloves

1 tsp ground nutmeg

½ tsp baking powder

1 cup shortening

1½ cups brown sugar

6 separated eggs

½ square of melted chocolate

¼ cup orange juice

¼ cup lemon juice

1. Preheat the oven to 300 degrees F, 150 degrees C or Gas Mark 2.

2. Grease a 10 inch (25cm) tube pan. Cut heavy waxed paper to fit the bottom and sides of the pan. Line the pan with waxed paper and lightly grease the paper in preparation.

3. Use a large bowl to mix together the cherries, peels, raisins, nuts, currants, citron, and pineapple, with 1 cup of flour to give them all a coating.

4. Use a medium bowl and mix together the remaining 1cup of flour, ground cinnamon, ground cloves, ground nutmeg, and baking powder.

5. Use an electric mixer bowl, blend together the shortening and brown sugar until fluffy. Add the egg yolks one by one, beating thoroughly after adding each one. Add the melted chocolate and beat.

6. Add the flour and spices mixture to the eggs mixture and thoroughly mix.

7. Add this mixture to the large bowl of floured fruit and nuts, adding the orange and lemon juice and thoroughly mix everything together.

8. Use a medium bowl to whisk the egg whites. When they are stiff gradually fold into the cake mixture.

9. Turn the mixture into the prepared cake tin and bake in the oven for 2 hours 20 minutes, until done and passes the cake tests.

10. Cool completely in the cake tin, then remove to an airtight container and store in a cool dry place for a few weeks to allow the flavors to richen.

Once the cake has cooled you may like to add rum or brandy (assuming the cake is only to be eaten by adults). To do this push a skewer into the top of the cake in several places, and fill the holes with the spirit.

47. White Christmas Cake

Serves 12

1 lb (455g) butter

1 oz (28g) lemon extract

6 separated eggs

2 cups sugar

1 lb (455g) white raisins

8oz (225g) candied green cherries

8oz (225g) candied red cherries

4oz (115g) candied chopped pineapple

1 lb (455g) halved pecans

3 cups plain flour

1. Preheat the oven to 300 degrees F, 150 degrees C or Gas Mark 2.

2. Grease and flour two, 9 inch (23cm) x 5 inch (13cm) x 3 inch (8cm) baking tins in preparation.

3. Use a large bowl to beat together the butter, lemon extract, egg yolks, and sugar, until creamy.

4. Add the fruit, nuts, and flour, and thoroughly mix together.

5. Use a small bowl and whisk the egg whites until stiff and fold into the cake mix.

6. Pour the mixture into the two prepared tins and bake for 1½ to 2 hours until cooked and pass the cake test. Turn off the oven and leave the cake there for 5 to 10 minutes before removing, to cool completely.

7. Wrap in foil and store in an airtight container in a cool dark place for a few weeks until ready to use.

48. Christmas Logs

Makes 45

1 cup butter

5 tbsp sugar

Pinch of salt

2 cups plain flour

1 tsp almond extract

1 tsp vanilla extract

¼ cup sugar

1½ tsp cinnamon

1. Preheat the oven to 300 degrees F, 150 degrees C or Gas Mark 2.

2. Use a medium bowl and mix together the butter, 5 tablespoons of sugar, salt, flour, almond extract, and the vanilla extract.

3. Lightly dust a flat even surface with flour and roll out the mixture into 2 inch (5cm) logs. (Should make approx 45)

4. Place the logs on a baking tray or sheet and bake for 15 to 20 minutes until done.

5. Use a small bowl and mix together the ¼ cup of sugar and cinnamon and roll the logs in the mixture to coat.

49. Apple Top Cake

Serves 6 to 8

½ cup shortening

¾ cup sugar

2 eggs

1 tsp vanilla

1¾ cup plain flour

3 tsp baking powder

¼ tsp salt

½ cup milk

1 cup sliced apples

¼ tsp cinnamon & sugar

1. Preheat the oven to 375 degrees F. 190 degrees C, or Gas Mark 5.

2. Grease a circular cake tin in preparation.

3. Use a medium bowl and mix together the shortening and sugar.

4. Add the eggs and vanilla and mix thoroughly.

5. Add the flour, baking powder, salt and milk and mix well.

6. Pour the mixture into the prepared baking tin. Place the apple slices on top of the mixture and sprinkle the cinnamon & sugar over it.

7. Bake in the oven for approximately 30 minutes until done.

50. Apple Sauce Cake

Serves 10

¾ cup shortening

2 cups sugar

3 eggs

3½ cups plain flour

4 tsp cinnamon

1 tsp nutmeg

½ tsp cloves

2 tsp baking powder

1 tsp salt

1 cup chopped pecans

1 lb (455g) raisins

1 lb (455g) sliced orange candy

3 cups apple sauce

1. Preheat the oven to 325 degrees F, 170 degrees C or Gas Mark 3.

2. Grease a large cake tin and line with grease proof paper in preparation.

3. Use a small bowl and cream together the shortening, sugar and eggs.

4. Use a medium bowl and mix together the flour, cinnamon, nutmeg, cloves, baking powder, and salt.

5. Add the egg mixture to the flour mixture and mix well.

6. Add the nuts, raisins, candied orange slices, and the applesauce, and thoroughly mix together.

7. Bake in the oven for 1½ hours until done.

51. Berlin Loaf

Serves 20

Cake

2 eggs

2 tbsp warm water

9 oz (255g) sugar

9 oz (255g) plain flour

1 tsp baking powder

4½ oz (125g) whole almonds

2½ oz (70g) apple preserve

2½ oz (70g) grated chocolate

1¼ oz (35g) chopped candied lemon peel

½ cup rum

3 tsp cinnamon

1 pinch of ground allspice

Icing

3½ oz (100g) confectioners sugar

1 – 2 tbsp hot water

1. Preheat the oven to 374 degrees f. 190 degrees C or Gas Mark 5.

2. Grease a baking sheet or tray in preparation.

Cake

3. Use a small bowl and whisk together the eggs and water until frothy. Gradually add the sugar and continue whisking until the mixture is thick and creamy.

4. Use a medium bowl and mix together the flour and baking powder.

5. Add the egg mixture to the flour mixture and mix together.

6. Gradually add the almonds, apple preserve, chocolate, candied lemon peel, rum, cinnamon, and allspice, and thoroughly mix.

7. Spread the mixture about ½ inch (5mm) thick on the baking sheet or tray.

8. Place the baking sheet or tray in the oven and bake for 15 to 20 minutes until done.

Icing

9. Use a small bowl or cup and mix the confectioners' sugar and water together to make the icing.

10. Spread the icing over the top of the cake whilst still hot and slice into 1 inch (25mm) x 2 inch (50mm) slices.

Recipe - 52. Coffee Nog

Serves 2

1 egg yolk

1 tbsp brown sugar

½ cup cream

8 fl oz (225ml) freshly brewed coffee

Ground nutmeg

1. Use a mug to beat together the egg yolk and sugar.

2. Use a small saucepan to heat the cream. Slowly add the egg mixture and when thoroughly blended, remove from the heat. Do not boil.

3. Pour coffee into your usual cups and top with the cream mixture, and nutmeg.

Part 2

Christmas Meals Made Easy

The holidays can be a stressful time for anyone. With all of the travel and relatives and parties, it can be a little overwhelming. If you are responsible for cooking the big meal, it can seem like almost too much. Thankfully, cooking a meal for a large group on Christmas or any other winter holiday can be a manageable and fun experience if you plan ahead and design the right menu.

The Christmas meal is important because it is one of the few times where we all sit down together for an extended meal with a large group of our friends and family. It's a time to reconnect and actually communicate in person. No family Christmas is ever perfect and sometimes it's those memories we talk about for years. But no matter how crazy the family drama is, you can always count on a good, hearty meal.

Christmas is a great time to splurge on a big piece of meat that you would not normally eat every day. These big cuts of meat taste great after a few hours in the oven, so you can easily start them in the morning and not stress over it. Many of the other dishes we eat at Christmas are similar to Thanksgiving dishes, like cranberry sauce, turkey, and mashed potatoes. However, Christmas has its own traditions as well. The Buche de Noel is a cake shaped like a log, which symbolizes the traditional Yule log burned on

Christmas. Eggnog is a thick and creamy drink that is flavored with vanilla and rum.

The most important thing to remember about cooking for Christmas is to pick a wide variety of dishes that will keep everyone happy during the meal. A Christmas meal should be comforting and warm and remind you of home. For some people, this will mean something strange like gelatin or fish (a traditional dish in Italy for Christmas), but don't be afraid to make room for these unique dishes at your table. If someone offers to bring something that is traditional for them, be open minded and willing to try something new. However, most people enjoy eating traditional dishes so it is a good idea not to get too crazy experimenting with new ideas. Make sure there are a few classic preparations of things like mashed potatoes or pumpkin pie.

The food you make doesn't have to be perfect, but thoughtful preparation will help make your dishes as good as they can possibly be. This book will help you choose recipes which are easy to follow and taste delicious. There are menus already planned for you with shopping lists, but you can always change out any dishes you don't like or add additional dishes.

Quick Tips for Holiday Meals

Planning the Menu

• Make a variety of dishes so everyone can get something they like.

• On an index card, write out the ingredient list for each dish. If someone has an allergy or is a vegetarian, they can easily look through the cards to determine what they can and can't eat.

• If making multiple dishes in the oven, plan out time for each so do not cook something at the wrong temperature.

• Lay out pans, serving platters, and casserole dishes to make sure you have enough. Borrow from friends or family if you need more.

• Start early. Go shopping at least a few days before and do some of the prep work one to two days ahead of time.

• If you do not cook often, either enlist the help of someone who does or make dishes that are within your comfort zone. Do not feel bad about taking help from the store or preparing simpler dishes.

Before Guests Arrive

• Ask for help – whether it means asking people bring a dish or two or asking for help when they arrive.

• Set the table the night before, including silverware, napkins, and glasses.

• Have small nibbles like nuts or crackers set around in small silver bowls.

• Set up a drink station so people can easily help themselves. Make sure to include non-alcoholic drinks like soda or water. Provide a way for people to identify their glasses, such as wine glass tags or colored bands.

• Play festive music.

• Light candles for greater ambiance. Use flameless candles if you have small children or pets around.

• Place nice, small trashcans around socializing areas, especially if you are using disposable cups or plates. Keep the large trashcan stashed away in the kitchen.

• 15 minutes before the party, pour yourself a drink and sit down. Even if everything isn't quite done, your calm demeanor will be more pleasant and guests won't complain about having to wait 10 more minutes to eat.

During the Party

• Be a good host. Introduce people who don't know each other and make sure to socialize with each guest.

• Don't apologize for the food. You worked hard to make it and even if it isn't perfect, people will still appreciate it. They will never see the mistakes unless you point them out!

• Have a fun after-dinner activity planned. If everyone is socializing well, it might not be needed, but it can give your guests something interesting to talk about.

• Have a designated spot for dirty dishes and silverware.

• Have small, disposable Tupperware available for guests to take home leftovers. You don't want to be eating turkey for the next two weeks!

• Leave the cleanup for after guests depart. If it's late, at least get everything soaking in hot soapy water.

Recipes

Appetizers

Bacon Dates

Ingredients

- 32 pitted dates (about 10 ounces)
- 2 ounces shelled, salted whole pistachios
- 2 ounces dried apricots, cut into 32 strips
- 1 pound lean bacon, strips cut in half

Instructions

1. Preheat oven to 450.
2. Cut a slit in the side of each date. Stuff with 2-3 pistachios and a slice of apricot.
3. Wrap each date in a half slice of bacon and secure with toothpick. Place on baking sheet.

4. Bake for about 10 minutes or until the bacon is crispy.

Oysters Rockefeller

Ingredients

- 3/4 cup firmly packed watercress sprigs, finely chopped
- 1 1/3 cups firmly packed baby spinach, finely chopped
- 3 tablespoons finely chopped scallion greens
- 1 tablespoon finely chopped fresh flat-leaf parsley
- 2 teaspoons minced celery
- 3 tablespoons coarse fresh bread crumbs
- 3 1/2 tablespoons unsalted butter
- 1 teaspoon Pernod or other anise-flavored liquor
- Pinch of cayenne
- 3 bacon slices
- About 10 cups kosher salt for baking and serving (3 lb)
- 20 small oysters on the half shell

Instructions

1. Mix first six ingredients in a bowl.
2. In a heavy skill over medium heat, melt butter, then add the spinach mixture. Sauté for 2 minutes or until greens are wilted.

3. Add Pernod, cayenne, and salt and pepper. Reduce liquid, then transfer back to bowl and chill for 1 hour.

4. Cook bacon in the same pan until crispy, then remove, crumble, and add to spinach mixture.

5. Preheat oven to 450.

6. In a large baking pan, spread kosher salt so the oyster shells can sit upright.

7. Spoon the spinach and bacon mixture over the oysters and sprinkle with remaining breadcrumbs.

8. Bake for 10 minutes, or until bread crumbs are golden brown.

Walnut Feta Cigars

Ingredients

- 6 ounces cream cheese, cut into pieces
- 6 ounces crumbled feta
- 2/3 cup walnut pieces
- 1/2 cup chopped pitted dates
- 1 (1 pound) package phyllo dough (17- by 12-inch sheets), thawed if frozen
- 10 tablespoons unsalted butter, melted and cooled slightly

Instructions

1. In a food processor, pulse cream cheese, feta, walnuts, and dates until the mixture is well combined.
2. Chill in freezer for 20 minutes.
3. Preheat oven to 400°F.
4. Stack the sheets of phyllo dough and cut them into 4 strips.
5. Place one strip of phyllo dough on your work surface. Lightly brush with butter.
6. Shape a tablespoon of cream cheese filling into a log shape, and then place it on the phyllo and roll like a cigar.

7. Place the roll on a baking sheet and repeat with remaining dough and filling.

8. Brush the tops of the rolls with butter.

9. Bake 15-20 minutes, or until the rolls are golden brown and crispy.

Cranberry Crab Rangoons

Ingredients

- Grapeseed or canola oil for cooking
- 2 red onions, cut into 1/2-inch dice
- 2 tablespoons minced lemongrass, white part only
- Kosher salt and freshly ground black pepper, to taste
- 2 cups dried cranberries, such as Craisins, chopped
- 1/2 cup sugar
- 2 cups rice vinegar
- 3 pounds picked, fresh crab meat
- 3/4 pound cream cheese, softened
- 1/2 cup chopped chives, 2 tablespoons reserved for garnish
- 1 package thin square wonton skins, defrosted (at least 60-count)
- 2 eggs mixed with 1/4 cup water

Instructions

1. In a medium sauté pan over high heat, cook onions and lemongrass for about 5 minutes, or until soft.
2. Deglaze the pan with rice vinegar; then add cranberries, sugar, and a pinch of salt.
3. Reduce until the liquid is nearly absorbed, then remove from heat and cool.

113

4. In a large bowl, mix crab, cream cheese, cranberry mixture and chives.

5. Place a wet paper towel over the wonton skins so they do not dry out during preparation.

6. Brush the edge of a wonton skin with the egg mixture, then place a spoonful of the cream cheese mixture in the middle. Top with a second wonton skin and seal the edges. Repeat with remaining wontons.

7. In a deep sauté pan, heat ¼ inch of oil over medium high-heat. Cook the wontons in small batches (do not crowd the pan) for 2-3 minutes per side, or until golden brown.

8. Garnish with remaining chives and serve immediately.

Pomegranate, Arugula, and Persimmon Salad

Ingredients

- 16 thin slices prosciutto (about 8 ounces)
- 1/2 cup fresh pomegranate seeds
- 1 large Fuyu persimmon, peeled, pitted, cut into 1/4-inch-thick slices
- 4 ounces baby arugula
- 1/2 cup pistachios, toasted
- Extra-virgin olive oil
- Pomegranate vinegar

Instructions

1. Mound arugula on a large serving platter.
2. Roll prosciutto into cones and place on arugula.
3. Scatter pomegranate seeds, persimmons, and pistachios over the lettuce.
4. Sprinkle with pepper; drizzle with oil and vinegar.

Crab Cakes

Ingredients

- Vinaigrette

o 1/2 cup grapeseed oil

o 1/4 cup fresh lemon juice

o 1 tablespoon minced fresh dill

o 1 tablespoon minced fresh tarragon

o 1 tablespoon minced fresh cilantro

o 1 tablespoon minced green onion

o 1/2 teaspoon Dijon mustard

- Crab cakes

o 1/4 cup mayonnaise

o 1/4 cup minced green onions

o 2 large egg yolks

o 2 tablespoons fresh lemon juice

o 4 teaspoons minced fresh dill

o 4 teaspoons minced fresh tarragon

o 4 teaspoons minced fresh cilantro

o 1 tablespoon Dijon mustard

o 1 tablespoon finely grated lemon peel

o 1/4 teaspoon ground black pepper

o 1 pound blue crabmeat or Dungeness crabmeat

o 2 cups panko, divided

o 2 tablespoons butter

o 2 tablespoons grapeseed oil

o 10 ounces herb salad mix

o Fresh dill sprigs

o Fresh tarragon sprigs

o Fresh cilantro sprigs

Instructions

1. Make vinaigrette. Whisk all ingredients in a small bowl and season with salt and pepper.

2. To make crab cakes, combine first 10 ingredients, and then add crab and one cup panko. Mix until thoroughly combined.

3. Form mixture into patties that are no larger than 2 inches in diameter.

4. Place remaining panko on a plate. Dip both sides of crab cake into the panko.

5. Chill crab cakes for at least 1 hour.

6. Melt butter and oil in a large skillet over high heat. Cook crab cakes for 2-3 minutes per side, or until golden brown.

7. Toss vinaigrette with salad and arrange on large platter. Place the crab cakes on top of the salad and drizzle with remaining vinaigrette.

Fingerlings with Crème Fraiche and Caviar

Ingredients

- 4 pounds unpeeled small fingerling potatoes, halved lengthwise
- 3 tablespoons olive oil
- 1 1/2 tablespoons minced fresh rosemary
- 1 1/2 cups chilled crème fraîche or sour cream
- 2 ounces black caviar (about 1/4 cup)

Instructions

1. Preheat oven to 400°F.
2. Combine potatoes, 2 tablespoons oil, salt, pepper, and rosemary in a bowl.
3. Arrange potatoes, cut side down, in single layer on prepared baking sheet.
4. Roast until potatoes are brown and crisp, about 35 minutes. Cool 10 minutes on sheet.
5. Place potatoes on serving platter. Drizzle with crème fraiche and place a small dollop of caviar on each potato wedge.

Prosciutto Quiche Cups

Ingredients

- 4 slices prosciutto, halved
- 2 egg whites
- 1 whole egg
- 3 tablespoons plain Greek yogurt
- 1 tablespoon chopped black olives
- 1/2 teaspoon chopped fresh rosemary, plus more for garnish
- 1/4 teaspoon salt
- 1/8 teaspoon freshly ground black pepper

Instructions

1. Preheat oven to 400°F.
2. Coat a mini muffin pan with cooking spray.
3. Press 1 piece prosciutto into each of 8 cups.
4. Combine remaining ingredients and whisk until smooth. Divide mixture among cups.
5. Bake for 10 minutes or until quiches are cooked through.

Chicken Skewers

Ingredients

- 8 skewers
- 3 tablespoons olive oil
- 2 1/2 teaspoons smoked paprika
- 1 teaspoon brown sugar
- 1 teaspoon salt
- 1/2 teaspoon black pepper
- 1 1/2 pounds chicken tenders (about 16 tenders), cut crosswise into 1-inch chunks
- 4 tangelos (or small oranges), peeled and segmented
- 1 medium red onion, cut into 1-inch chunks

Instructions

1. Preheat oven to 450.
2. In a small bowl, combine oil, paprika, sugar, salt, and pepper.
3. Thread chicken, tangelos and onion onto skewers, alternating pieces.
4. Place skewers on a baking sheet and brush with oil mixture.
5. Bake for 10-12 minutes or until chicken is cooked through.

Artichoke Dip

Ingredients

- 3 cans (14 ounces each) artichoke hearts in water, chopped
- 6 tablespoons unsalted butter, room temperature
- 1/4 cup all-purpose flour
- 2 cups whole milk, warmed
- 2 teaspoons coarse salt
- Freshly ground black pepper, to taste
- 1/8 teaspoon cayenne pepper
- 1 1/2 teaspoons finely grated lemon zest
- 1 cup grated Parmesan cheese (3 ounces)
- 1 cup grated pecorino cheese (3 ounces)
- 1 large onion, finely chopped
- 1 tablespoon fresh thyme leaves, chopped, plus leaves for garnish
- 3 garlic cloves, minced
- 1/4 cup fresh breadcrumbs
- Sliced vegetables and crackers for serving

Instructions

1. Preheat oven to 400.

2. In a sauce pan over medium heat, melt 4 tablespoons of butter. Add flour and cook for 2 minutes. Whisk in milk; bring to a simmer. Cook for 3-5 minutes or until slightly thickened. Remove from heat and add salt, pepper, cayenne, lemon zest, and cheese.

3. Melt remaining butter. Add onion, thyme, garlic, and artichokes and cook for 3-5 minutes. Add to cheese mixture.

4. Transfer to large baking dish and sprinkle with breadcrumbs.

5. Bake for 15 minutes or until golden brown and bubbly.

Sides

Spicy Cranberry Sauce

Ingredients

- 1 tablespoon vegetable oil
- 2 cups cranberries (about 8 ounces)
- 1 tablespoon minced fresh ginger
- 2 cups Pinot Noir or other dry red wine
- 1 1/2 cups sugar
- 3 tablespoons chopped crystallized ginger
- 1 teaspoon curry powder
- 1 teaspoon of Chinese five-spice powder

Instructions

1. In a large skillet, heat oil over medium high heat. Add cranberries and ginger and cook until cranberries start to burst, about 4 minutes.

124

2. Add wine and sugar. Simmer for 15 minutes or until reduced to 2 cups.

3. Add remaining spices. Add salt and pepper to taste.

4. Can be served cold or warmed over low heat.

Carrots with Citrus

Ingredients

- 1 pound carrots, cut into 1-inch pieces
- ½
- cup plus 2 tablespoons extra-virgin olive oil
- Kosher salt and freshly ground black pepper
- 1/4 cup freshly squeezed orange juice
- 1/4 cup Champagne vinegar
- 2 tablespoons honey
- 1 tablespoon minced shallots

Instructions

1. Preheat the oven to 400 °F
2. Place carrots on a baking sheet and coat with olive oil, salt and pepper. Bake for 20 minutes.
3. Meanwhile, combine the remaining ingredients and whisk to combine.
4. While carrots are still hot, mix with the dressing. Serve warm or cold.

Cherry Walnut Green Beans

Ingredients

- 1/3 cup extra-virgin olive oil
- 1/3 cup minced shallots
- 3 tablespoons plus 2 teaspoons Sherry wine vinegar
- 2 tablespoons chopped fresh mint
- 1 1/2 teaspoons coarse kosher salt
- 1 teaspoon sugar
- 1/2 teaspoon black pepper
- 1/3 cup dried tart cherries
- 1 1/2 pounds trimmed slender green beans
- 1/2 cup walnuts, toasted, chopped

Instructions

1. To make dressing, whisk together first 7 ingredients.
2. Shock green beans in salted boiling water for 3-4 minutes.
3. Toss green beans, cherries, and walnuts with dressing. Can be served warm or cold.

Sausage and Bread Stuffing

Ingredients

- 8 cups bread cubes (1 large loaf)
- 2 tablespoons olive oil, divided
- 2 pounds sweet Italian sausage, casings removed, divided
- 1 stick unsalted butter, cut into pieces
- 3 medium onions, chopped
- 4 large celery ribs, chopped
- 5 garlic cloves, minced
- 4 large eggs, lightly beaten
- 3/4 cup heavy cream, divided
- 1/2 cup turkey giblet stock or reduced-sodium chicken broth
- 1 cup grated Parmigiano-Reggiano (2 ounces)
- 1/2 cup coarsely chopped flat-leaf parsley

Instructions

1. Preheat oven to 350 °F.
2. Grease two 4-qt glass baking dishes.
3. Place bread cubes in a single layer on a baking sheet and bake for 10 minutes. When bread is done, raise the heat to 425 °F.

4. In a large skillet, heat olive oil over medium-high heat. Cook sausage until it is golden brown. Remove sausage to a separate plate.

5. Reduce heat to medium. Cook onions, celery, garlic, along with salt and pepper, in butter until golden brown and softened, about 15 minutes.

6. Combine bread cubes, sausage, and vegetable mixture and place in baking dishes.

7. Combine remaining ingredients, whisk until smooth, then pour over stuffing. Let sit for 30 minutes.

8. Bake covered for 20 minutes. Remove foil and cook for an additional 20 minutes or until top is golden brown and crisp.

Mashed Potatoes with Garlic Gravy

Ingredients

4 pounds Yukon gold potatoes

8 tablespoons butter, cut into pieces

4-6 garlic cloves, chopped 5 tablespoons unsalted butter

2 tablespoons butter

2 tablespoons olive oil

1/4 tablespoons all-purpose flour

1/4 cup milk

1/4 cup chicken stock or water

Instructions

1. Cut potatoes into two inch pieces. Place in saucepan and cover with water. Add a few teaspoons of salt.

2. Bring to a simmer and cook for 15-20 minutes. Drain. Add 8 tablespoons of butter and salt to taste. Coarsely mash potatoes.

3. While potatoes are cooking, make the gravy. In a saucepan, melt remaining 2 tablespoons of butter and olive oil over medium heat. Add chopped garlic and cook until golden brown.

4. Sprinkle flour over butter and let cook for 3-5 minutes. Whisk in milk and chicken stock and salt to taste. Pour gravy over mashed potatoes.

Winter Vegetable Bake

Ingredients

- 2 cups 1/2-inch cubes peeled kabocha squash (about 1 1/2 pounds)
- 2 cups 1/2-inch cubes peeled butternut squash (about 1 1/2 pounds)
- 2 cups 1/4- to 1/3-inch cubes peeled parsnips (about 12 ounces)
- 5 tablespoons butter
- 1/2 cup pure maple syrup
- 2 garlic cloves, minced
- 1 1/2 tablespoons chopped fresh rosemary
- 1 teaspoon salt
- 1/2 teaspoon freshly ground black pepper
- 3/4 cup coarsely chopped Marcona almonds (about 3 1/2 ounces)

Instructions

1. Place chopped squashes in a 11x7 glass baking dish.
2. In a small saucepan, add all remaining ingredients except almonds. Cook over low heat until melted and combined. Pour over squash.

3. Bake covered for 30 minutes, then uncover and continue cooking for another 30 minutes or until vegetables are soft.

4. Sprinkle with almonds.

Savory Sweet Potatoes

Ingredients

- 8 slender medium garnet yams or other yams (red-skinned sweet potatoes; about 5 pounds total), rinsed, dried
- 1 stick unsalted butter
- 1 small shallot, peeled
- 1 garlic clove, peeled
- 1 teaspoon coarse kosher salt plus additional for seasoning
- 1 tablespoon Dijon mustard
- 1 1/2 tablespoons red wine vinegar

Instructions

1. Preheat oven to 400 °F.
2. Bake yams for 45 minutes or until almost soft.
3. While the yams are baking, make the vinaigrette. Melt butter over medium heat in a saucepan until lightly browned. Whisk together with remaining ingredients and season to taste.
4. Cut the cooked sweet potatoes into round slices and drizzle with vinaigrette.

Rice with Winter Vegetables

Ingredients

- 1 1/2 cups wild rice (about 9 ounces)
- 2 teaspoons coarse kosher salt
- 3 cups 1/2-inch cubes peeled butternut squash (from 11/2-pound squash)
- 3 tablespoons olive oil
- 6 tablespoons (3/4 stick) butter, divided
- 1 1/2 cups finely chopped leeks (white part only)
- 1 1/2 cups frozen white corn kernels, thawed
- 1 tablespoon chopped fresh Italian parsley

Instructions

1. Bring 6 cups of water to a boil. Add rice and salt, reduce heat to simmer, and cook for 45 minutes or until rice is tender. Drain and spread rice on baking sheet to cool.

2. Preheat oven to 350°F. Toss squash cubes and 3 tablespoons oil in medium bowl. Sprinkle with salt and pepper. Roast for 15 minutes.

3. Melt 4 tablespoons butter in large skillet over medium heat. Add leeks and 3/4 cup water; simmer for 7 minutes. Add corn; simmer 2 minutes longer.

Add rice and butternut squash; simmer until heated through and liquid is absorbed, about 4 minutes.

4. Stir in butter and parsley. Season with salt and pepper. Transfer to bowl and serve.

Mixed potato gratin

Ingredients

- 3 pounds mixed russet potatoes and sweet potatoes
- Butter for baking dish and foil
- 1 1/2 cups heavy whipping cream
- 1/2 cup chicken broth
- 1 tablespoon chopped sage
- 1 minced garlic clove
- 1 teaspoon kosher salt
- ground black pepper
- 1 cup grated Gruyère cheese

Instructions

1. Preheat oven to 425°F.
2. Cut potatoes into slices and layer in 11x7 baking dish.
3. Combine cream, broth, and seasonings and pour over potatoes.
4. Cover with foil and bake for 40 minutes.
5. Remove foil, top with shredded cheese, and baking for an additional 30 minutes.
6. Let cool before serving.

Garlic Mushrooms

Ingredients

- 1 cup small bread cubes
- 3 tablespoons unsalted butter
- 1 tablespoon finely chopped garlic
- 1/2 teaspoon salt
- 1/4 teaspoon black pepper
- 3/4 lb small white mushrooms
- 2 tablespoons finely chopped fresh flat-leaf parsley

Instructions

1. Preheat oven to 375°F.
2. Toast bread cubes in oven for 10 minutes or until lightly crisp.
3. Melt butter with garlic, salt, and pepper. Toss with mushrooms. Bake for 20 minutes or until mushrooms are soft.
4. Top with croutons and parsley before serving.

Mains

Herbed Lamb Leg

Ingredients

- One 7- to 8-pound leg of lamb
- 1/2 cup rosemary leaves, minced
- 1 teaspoon thyme leaves
- 3 garlic cloves, finely chopped
- 2 tablespoons Dijon mustard
- 1/3 cup extra-virgin olive oil
- 1/2 cup honey
- Salt
- Freshly ground black pepper

Instructions

1. Preheat the oven to 500°.

2. In a food processor, pulse the rosemary, thyme, garlic, mustard, olive oil and honey. Season with salt and pepper.

3. Season the lamb with salt and pepper. Spread 1 tablespoon of the herb mustard inside of the lamb. Roll up the meat and tie with kitchen string. Rub the lamb roast with the remaining herb mustard.

4. Set the lamb on a wire rack in a roasting pan. Add 1 cup of water to the pan. Turn down the oven to 375° and roast the lamb for about 90 minutes, or until the internal temperature reaches 130°.

5. Let the lamb rest for 15 minutes, then remove the string, slice and serve.

Apple Walnut Pork Roast

Ingredients

- 5 tablespoons butter
- 1 apple - peeled, cored, and chopped
- 1 small onion, chopped
- 1 celery stalk, diced
- 1/2 cup chopped walnuts
- 1 cup unsweetened applesauce
- 1 1/2 cups water
- 5 cups dry bread crumbs
- 1/2 teaspoon ground cinnamon
- 1/2 teaspoon kosher salt
- 1/4 teaspoon ground cloves
- 1/4 teaspoon ground nutmeg
- 1/4 teaspoon ground ginger
- 1 (3 pound) boneless rolled pork loin roast

Instructions

1. Preheat oven to 325°F.
2. Melt butter in a saucepan. Add apple, onion, celery, and walnuts and cook for 5 minutes. Add applesauce, water, breadcrumbs, and seasonings.

141

3. Lay roast flat and spoon stuffing on top. Roll and secure with twine.

4. Bake 45 minutes or until the internal temperature is 145°F.

5. Let rest for 10 minutes before slicing and serving.

Maple Roast Pork

Ingredients

- 2 1/2 pounds boneless pork loin roast
- 1 cup real maple syrup
- 4 tablespoons prepared Dijon-style mustard
- 2 1/2 tablespoons cider vinegar
- 2 1/2 tablespoons soy sauce
- salt
- ground black pepper

Instructions

1. Preheat oven to 350°F.
2. Place pork in a shallow roasting pan.
3. Combine remaining ingredients and spread over pork.
4. Bake for 1 hour or until the internal temperature is 145°F.
5. Let rest for 10 minutes before slicing and serving.

Apricot Ham

Ingredients

- 1 (10 pound) fully-cooked spiral cut ham
- 2/3 cup brown sugar
- 1/3 cup apricot jam
- 1 teaspoon dry mustard powder

Instructions

1. Preheat the oven to 275°F.
2. Place ham cut side down in large roasting dish.
3. Combine remaining ingredients and spread half of the glaze over ham.
4. Bake for 2 hours or about 14 minutes per pound if the ham is a different size.
5. Raise heat to 350°F and apply remaining half of glaze to ham. Cook for an additional 20 minutes.
6. Let rest for 10 minutes before slicing.

Baked Salmon

Ingredients

- 3 tablespoons Dijon mustard
- 3 tablespoons butter, melted
- 5 teaspoons honey
- 1/2 cup fresh bread crumbs
- 1/2 cup finely chopped pecans
- 3 teaspoons chopped fresh parsley
- 6 (4 ounce) fillets salmon
- salt and pepper to taste
- 6 lemon wedges

Instructions

1. Preheat oven to 400.
2. In one small bowl, mix together mustard, butter, and honey. In another small bowl, mix together breadcrumbs, pecan, and parsley.
3. Place the salmon filets in a baking dish. Cover with honey mustard, then sprinkle breadcrumb mixture on top.
4. Bake for 10 minutes per inch or until salmon just flakes.
5. Serve immediately with lemon wedges.

145

Ham with Riesling and Mustard

Ingredients

- 1 14–16-pound whole cured, smoked bone-in ham
- 2 cups sweet (Auslese) Riesling, divided
- 2 tablespoons (1/4 stick) unsalted butter
- 1/4 cup finely chopped shallots
- 3 sprigs thyme plus 2 teaspoons fresh thyme leaves
- 1/2 cup whole grain mustard
- 1 tablespoon honey
- 1/2 teaspoon freshly ground black pepper
- Small pinch of kosher salt

Instructions

1. Preheat oven to 300°F.
2. Score ham fat crosswise (do not cut into meat) on top of ham with parallel cuts to make diamond shapes.
3. Place ham in a large roasting rack pan.
4. Boil 1 cup Riesling and 7 cups water in a saucepan for 5 minutes. Pour over ham and bake for about 3 hours. Baste the ham with pan juices occasionally, until an internal temperature reaches 110°F.
5. Meanwhile, melt butter in a skillet over medium heat. Add shallots and thyme and cook until shallots

are soft, about 10 minutes. Add remaining 1 cup Riesling. Bring to a simmer and cook until reduced to 1/4 cup, about 10 minutes.

6. Remove the thyme sprigs and transfer mixture to a food processor. Add thyme leaves, mustard, honey, pepper, and salt. Process until well blended.

7. Remove ham from oven and increase heat to 350°F. Spread Riesling mixture over ham. Return pan to oven and bake for an additional 30 minutes.

8. Let rest before slicing.

Bacon and Spinach Stuffed Ribeye

Ingredients

Stuffing:

- 1 pound sliced applewood-smoked bacon, chopped
- 1/2 cup finely chopped celery
- 1/2 cup finely chopped shallots
- 3 garlic cloves, chopped
- 2 1/2 cups cooked (or three 10-ounce bags frozen, thawed) spinach, squeezed dry, finely chopped
- 1/4 cup crème fraîche or sour cream
- 2 cups coarse fresh breadcrumbs made from day-old white bread
- 1/2 cup finely chopped scallions
- 1 teaspoon chopped fresh sage
- 1 teaspoon chopped fresh thyme
- 1/4 teaspoon nutmeg, preferably freshly grated
- Kosher salt and freshly ground black pepper
- 2 large eggs, whisked to blend

Roast:

- 1 5-bone standing beef rib-eye roast (10–13 pounds), chine bone removed, fat trimmed to 1/4" thickness
- Kosher salt and freshly ground black pepper

- 2 tablespoons olive oil
- 1/4 cup finely chopped fresh thyme

Instructions

1. Cook bacon over medium heat until bacon is browned, about 10 minutes. Remove bacon from pan and set aside.

2. Add celery, shallots, and garlic; cook 5 minutes until vegetables are soft. Add spinach and crème fraiche and cook for 2–3 minutes longer. Remove to large bowl.

3. Add breadcrumbs, scallions, sage, thyme, and nutmeg into stuffing mixture. Season with salt and pepper

4. Preheat oven to 450°F.

5. Cut roast to create a 3"–4"-wide pocket at the top. Lightly pack stuffing into pocket. Starting at one end, tie kitchen twine horizontally around the bones to keep them in place and secure the stuffing.

6. Season the roast with olive oil, thyme, salt, and pepper.

7. Roast beef for 20 minutes.

8. Reduce heat to 350°F and continue roasting for about 3 hours or until the internal temperature of the thickest part of roast registers 110°F–115°F for rare and 120°F–125°F for medium-rare.

9. Let rest for at least 20 minutes and up to 1 hour. Remove the twine. Slice and serve.

Shortribs with Cranberry Sauce

Ingredients

- 15 pounds beef short ribs, cut into 3- to 4-inch pieces
- 4 teaspoons kosher salt
- 2 1/2 teaspoons freshly ground black pepper
- 2 tablespoons canola oil
- 5 large onions, roughly chopped (about 5 cups)
- 6 carrots, roughly chopped (about 3 1/2 cups)
- 1/2 bunch celery, roughly chopped (about 3 cups)
- 2 medium fennel bulbs roughly chopped
- 4 lemongrass stalks, root ends trimmed, tough outer leaves discarded, and finely chopped
- 3 tablespoons garlic, minced (about 6 to 7 cloves)
- 1 tablespoon ginger, minced (from 1/2-inch knob)
- 4 cups rice wine or sake
- 2 cups dark soy sauce
- 1 cup cranberry sauce
- 6 whole sprigs fresh thyme
- 3 dried bay leaves

Instructions

1. Sprinkle short ribs with salt and pepper. Working in batches, sear the short ribs in a large pan over

medium high heat until all sides are brown. Set aside.

2. Add vegetables to pan and cook for 10 minutes or until soft. Add remaining ingredients and bring to a boil.

3. Add short ribs, reduce heat to low, and simmer for 3 to 4 hours or until short ribs are falling apart.

Pork Roast with Winter Fruit and Port

Ingredients

For stuffing:

- 1/4 pound California dried apricots, cut into 1/2-inch pieces
- 1/4 pound pitted prunes, cut into 1/2-inch pieces
- 2/3 cup ruby Port
- 1 medium onion, finely chopped
- 1 small shallot, finely chopped
- 3/4 stick unsalted butter
- 1 tart apple such as Granny Smith, peeled and cut into 1/2-inch pieces

For roast:

- 1 (6-pound) bone-in pork loin roast (10 ribs), frenched, at room temperature 1 hour
- 9 or 10 bacon slices

For port sauce:

- 1/2 cup ruby Port
- 1 small shallot, finely chopped
- 1 1/2 cups water, divided
- 2 teaspoons arrowroot

Instructions

153

1. Make the stuffing. In a pan over medium heat, sauté the onions and shallots in butter for 5 minutes. Add apple, salt, and pepper and continue cooking for 5 minutes.

2. Meanwhile, simmer apricots, prunes, and port in a small pan for 5 minutes. Add to vegetable mixture. Set aside.

3. Preheat oven to 500°F.

4. Make a pocket in center of roast by making a horizontal 1 1/2-inch-wide cut into 1 end of roast. Push about 1 cup stuffing into pocket using a long-handled spoon.

5. Season outside of roast with salt and pepper, then wrap in bacon.

6. Roast for 20 minutes, then reduce the heat to 325°F and cook for another 45 minutes, or until the internal temperature reaches 155°F. Let cool for 30 minutes.

7. While pork is cooling, make the sauce. Sauté shallot in butter until soft. Add 1 tablespoon of pan drippings, 1 cup water, and port, and bring to a boil. Whisk together arrowroot and ½ cup water, then add to mixture. Simmer until sauce is thickened.

Slow Roasted Balsamic Duck

Ingredients

2 (4 1/2-pound) Long Island or Peking ducks

Coarse sea salt and freshly ground pepper

6 tablespoons olive oil

2 heads garlic

4 bulbs fennel, chopped

6 cups store-bought low-sodium chicken stock

1 lemon, halved crosswise

1 bunch thyme

1 cup balsamic vinegar

Juice of 1 lemon

Instructions

1. Preheat oven to 350°F.

2. Season duck with thyme and salt. Stuff with lemon halves. Roast for 2-3 hours.

3. Mix together lemon juice and balsamic. Every 30 minutes, baste duck with this mixture.

4. To make sauce, heat a sauté pan over medium heat. Cook garlic and fennel in olive oil until soft. Add chicken stock and simmer until reduced by half. Set aside.

5. Let stand for 15 minutes before serving.

Prime Rib

Ingredients

- 1 three-rib prime roast, first cut, trimmed and tied
- 1 tablespoon freshly ground black pepper
- 2 tablespoons salt
- 1 1/2 cups dry red wine

Instructions

1. Preheat oven to 450°F.
2. Season roast with salt and pepper and place fat side up in a roasting pan.
3. Cook for 20 minutes, then reduce oven temperature to 325 °F and continue cooking for about an hour, or until the internal temperature is 115 °F.
4. Set roast aside to rest for 20 minutes.
5. Meanwhile, pour juices out of pan. Use a fat separator to remove the fat from the juices.
6. Pour red wine into pan and simmer until reduced by half. Add the fatless pan juices and simmer for an additional 5 minutes. Strain and serve on the side.

Drinks

Eggnog

Ingredients

- 4 cups milk
- 5 whole cloves
- 1/2 teaspoon vanilla extract
- 1 teaspoon ground cinnamon
- 12 egg yolks
- 1 1/2 cups sugar
- 2 1/2 cups light rum
- 4 cups light cream
- 2 teaspoons vanilla extract
- 1/2 teaspoon ground nutmeg

Instructions

1. Combine milk, vanilla, and cinnamon in a small saucepan over medium-low heat. Bring to a simmer, then turn off heat.

2. In a large bowl, mix eggs and sugar until fluffy. Add half of the hot milk to the eggs and combine. Pour into saucepan with the rest of milk and cook over medium heat for about 3 minutes or until thick. Do not boil.

3. Add remaining ingredients and chill overnight. Strain before serving.

Hot Cocoa

Ingredients

- 2 cups powdered sugar
- 1 cup cocoa (Dutch-process preferred)
- 2 1/2 cups powdered milk
- 1 teaspoon salt
- 2 teaspoons cornstarch
- 1 pinch cayenne pepper, or more to taste
- Hot water

Instructions

1. Combine all ingredients and incorporate evenly.
2. When ready to serve, heat 4 to 6 cups of water or milk.
3. Fill a mug half full with the cocoa mixture and pour in hot liquid. Stir to combine.
4. Seal the rest in an airtight container, keeps indefinitely in the pantry.

Cava and Pomegranate

Ingredients

- Seeds from 1 pomegranate
- Two 750-milliliter bottles cava or other sparkling dry white wine, chilled
- 1/4 cup pomegranate juice

Instructions

1. Fill 12 flutes with cava.
2. Add 1 teaspoon of the pomegranate juice to each flute, garnish with pomegranate seeds and serve.

161

Irish Cream

Ingredients

- 1 cup heavy cream
- 1 (14 ounce) can sweetened condensed milk
- 1 2/3 cups Irish whiskey
- 1 teaspoon instant coffee granules
- 2 tablespoons chocolate syrup
- 1 teaspoon vanilla extract
- 1 teaspoon almond extract

Instructions

1. Blend all ingredients for 30 seconds. Store in a tightly sealed container in the refrigerator. Shake well before serving.

Hot Apple Cider

Ingredients

- 6 cups apple cider
- 1/4 cup real maple syrup
- 2 cinnamon sticks
- 6 whole cloves
- 6 whole allspice berries
- 1 orange peel, cut into strips
- 1 lemon peel, cut into strips

Instructions

1. Place apple cider and maple syrup in large pot.
2. Places spices in a tea strainer or cheesecloth. Drop the bundle into the cider mixture.
3. Heat for 15-20 minutes over low heat, or until the cider is just simmering.
4. Remove from heat and ladle into mugs.

Cranberry Wassail

Ingredients

- 1/2 gallon apple cider
- 1/2 gallon cranberry juice
- 1 cup lemon juice
- 1 1/4 cups pineapple juice
- 1 large orange, thinly sliced
- 24 whole cloves
- 1/4 cup clover honey
- 1/2 cup white sugar
- 4 cinnamon sticks
- 1 teaspoon ground nutmeg
- 1 teaspoon ground allspice
- 1/2 teaspoon ground ginger
- 12 fresh mint leaves for garnish
- 12 orange slices for garnish

Instructions

1. Combine all ingredients in a large pot. Simmer for 20 minutes.
2. Serve warm and garnish with mint and orange.

Poinsettia Cocktail

Ingredients

- Champagne
- 1/2 ounce Cointreau
- 3 ounces cranberry juice

Instructions

1. Mix Cointreau and cranberry juice; add to chilled champagne flute. Fill the rest of the glass with champagne.

Hot Buttered Rum Punch

Ingredients

- 1 bottle of dark rum
- 1 stick of soft butter
- 2 cups of brown sugar
- 1/2 teaspoon ground nutmeg
- 1 teaspoon ground cinnamon
- a pinch of ground cloves
- a pinch of salt
- boiling water

Instructions

1. Cream butter, sugar, and spices in a mixer. Refrigerate until firm.
2. Spoon two tablespoons of butter into mugs. Add 3 oz of water and 3 oz of rum to each mug.
3. Stir well and serve warm.

Mulled Wine

Ingredients

- 1 bottle red wine
- 1 cup cognac
- 3/4 cup sugar
- 2 cinnamon sticks
- 3 whole cloves
- 1 tsp grated nutmeg
- 1 vanilla bean
- 1 star anise
- 1 sliced orange
- 1 sliced lemon

Instructions

1. Combine all ingredients in a pot and simmer for 25 minutes over low heat.
2. Let it sit overnight.
3. Strain wine and serve.

Chocolate Raspberry Martini

Ingredients

- 3 Ounces Vodka
- 1 1/2 Ounces Creme De Cacao
- 3/4 Ounce Raspberry Liqueur
- 3/4 Ounce Kahlua
- Fresh Raspberry
- Ice

Instructions

1. Combine all ingredients in shaker. Shake until well combined.
2. Serve in chilled martini glass with fresh raspberries.

Desserts

Candy Cane Fudge

Ingredients

- 2 (10 ounce) packages vanilla baking chips
- 1 (14 ounce) can sweetened condensed milk
- 1/2 teaspoon peppermint extract
- 1 1/2 cups crushed candy canes
- 1 dash red or green food coloring

Instructions

1. Line an 8x8 baking dish with aluminum foil, then grease the foil.
2. Melt vanilla chips and milk in a saucepan over medium-low heat. Stir until smooth, then remove from heat and add remaining ingredients.

169

3. Add to dish and chill for at least 3 hours before serving.

Buche de Noel

Ingredients

- 2 cups heavy cream
- 1/2 cup powdered sugar
- 1/2 cup unsweetened cocoa powder
- 1 teaspoon vanilla extract
- 6 egg yolks
- 1/2 cup white sugar
- 1/3 cup unsweetened cocoa powder
- 1 1/2 teaspoons vanilla extract
- 1/8 teaspoon salt
- 6 egg whites
- 1/4 cup white sugar
- confectioners' sugar for dusting

Instructions

1. Preheat oven to 375 °F.
2. Line an 11x18 baking sheet (jelly roll pan) with parchment paper.
3. Whip cream, powdered sugar, cocoa powder, and vanilla until stiff peaks form. Chill.
4. Cream egg yolks and sugar until thick. Add cocoa, vanilla, and salt. Set aside.

171

5. Beat egg whites until soft peaks form, then add sugar and beat until stiff peaks form. Fold into the yolk mixture and spread evenly in baking sheet.

6. Bake for 15 minutes.

7. Dust a thin dish towel with powdered sugar. Turn cake out onto towel and roll into a log. Chill for 30 minutes.

8. Unroll the log and remove the dishtowel. Spread filling on the inside of the cake and reroll. Place seam side down and refrigerate.

9. Cut cake into slices and dust with powdered sugar.

Perfect Peanut Butter Cookies

Ingredients

- 1 3/4 cups all-purpose flour
- 1 teaspoon baking soda
- 1/2 teaspoon salt
- 1 cup sugar
- 1/2 cup packed dark brown sugar
- 8 tablespoons (1 stick) unsalted butter, cut into small pieces
- 1/2 cup smooth or chunky peanut butter (not natural)
- 1 large egg
- 1 teaspoon pure vanilla or almond extract
- 30 chocolate kisses, unwrapped

Instructions

1. Preheat oven to 350 °F.
2. Sift together flour, baking soda, and salt.
3. In a mixer, combine sugars, butter, and peanut butter. Beat for 3-4 minutes, then add in egg and vanilla and beat for an additional 2 minutes.
4. Slowly add in the flour mixture and stir until just combined.

5. Roll dough into 1 inch balls and roll in sugar.

6. Bake on a cookie sheet for 8-10 minutes.

7. Press a chocolate kiss into the center of each cookie and let cool for 10 minutes.

Maple Pecan Pie

Ingredients

- 3/4 cup pure maple syrup
- 3/4 cup (packed) golden brown sugar
- 1/2 cup light corn syrup
- 1/4 cup (1/2 stick) unsalted butter
- Prepared unbaked pie crust
- 3 large eggs
- 1 teaspoon vanilla extract
- 1/4 teaspoon salt
- 1 1/2 cups pecan halves

Instructions

1. Combine maple syrup, corn syrup, sugar, and butter in a saucepan over medium-high heat and boil for 1 minute. Let cool.

2. Place pecan halves in chilled unbaked pie shell.

3. Whisk together eggs, vanilla, and salt, then add to maple syrup mixture.

4. Pour oven pecan halves.

5. Bake for 1 hour or until pie is set in the middle. Cool completely before serving.

Chocolate Pecan Tarts

Ingredients

- 5 tablespoons butter, softened, plus 1 tablespoon melted butter
- 4 ounces light cream cheese
- 1 cup all-purpose flour
- 1 tablespoon confectioners' sugar
- 1/2 teaspoon salt, divided
- 3/4 cup light-brown sugar
- 1/3 cup mini semisweet chocolate chips
- 1 large egg
- 1 teaspoon vanilla extract
- 2/3 cup chopped pecans

Instructions

1. Mix softened butter and cream cheese until smooth. Add flour, confectioners' sugar, and salt. Form into a disc and refrigerate for at least 4 hours.
2. Preheat oven to 325°F.
3. Divide dough into 24 balls. Press into a mini muffin tin to form the crust. Chill.
4. While crusts are chilling, mix brown sugar, chocolate, egg, melted butter, vanilla, and salt.

5. Place a few pecan pieces in each crust, then cover with brown sugar mixture.

6. Bake 20 minutes or until dough is golden brown.

7. Cool completely before serving.

Cider-Poached Apples with Candied Walnuts and Rum Cream

Ingredients

For apples:

- 6 medium Gala apples (about 3 pounds), peeled and cored
- 1/2 lemon
- 1/2 gallon apple cider
- 1 cup packed light brown sugar

For candied walnuts:

- 1 cup chopped walnuts (4 ounces)
- 2 tablespoons granulated sugar
- 1 tablespoon unsalted butter, melted
- 1 large egg white, lightly beaten

For cream:

- 1/2 cup chilled heavy cream
- 1 1/2 tablespoon granulated sugar
- 1 tablespoon dark rum
- 1/4 teaspoon pure vanilla extract

Instructions

1. Place apples in a wide pan and cover with cider and brown sugar. Rub any apple exposed to the air with lemon.

2. Bring mixture to a boil over medium heat, cover, and cook for 30 minutes.

3. Remove from heat and cool apples in the cider for 1 hour.

4. Meanwhile, make the nuts and cream.

5. For the walnuts, preheat the oven to 450°F. Mix together all ingredients and toast for 5 minutes or until golden brown. Let cool.

6. For the cream, beat together all ingredients until the cream forms medium stiff peaks.

7. When ready to serve, drain apples. Sprinkle each with candied walnuts and top with whipped cream.

Zeppole

Ingredients

Sauce:

- 8 ounces 70% bittersweet chocolate, chopped
- 1 cup heavy whipping cream
- 1/4 cup honey

Zeppole:

- 2 cups plus 1/2 tablespoon bread flour
- 1/2 cup plus 1/2 tablespoon whole milk
- 3 tablespoons sugar
- 1 1/2 teaspoons lemon zest
- 3/4 teaspoon active dry yeast (from 1 envelope)
- 3/4 teaspoon fine sea salt
- 2 large eggs
- 3/4 cup (1 1/2 stick) unsalted butter, room temperature, cut into cubes
- Vegetable oil (for deep-frying)
- Powdered sugar

1. Make the dough. Combine flour, milk, sugar, lemon zest, yeast, salt, and eggs in a mixer until dough forms. Slowly add the butter until absorbed. Beat for 5 minutes, then cover with plastic wrap and let rise for two hours.

2. Meanwhile, make the sauce. Combine cream and honey over medium heat until it just bubbles, then pour over chopped chocolate. Stir to combine.

3. To make donuts, heat frying oil to 325°F. Drop 1 inch pieces of dough and fry until golden brown, about 4 minutes. Transfer to paper towels and dust with powdered sugar.

4. Serve warm with chocolate sauce.

Fruitcake Trifle

Ingredients

- 1/2 cup plus 3 tablespoons dark brown sugar, packed
- 3 tablespoons light butter
- 1 egg
- 1 teaspoon pure vanilla extract
- 3/4 cup all-purpose flour
- 1 teaspoon cinnamon
- 3/4 teaspoon baking powder
- 1/4 teaspoon salt
- 1/4 teaspoon ground ginger
- 1/8 teaspoon ground cloves
- 1/3 cup plain Greek yogurt
- 1/4 cup hazelnuts
- 1 cup cream
- 1/4 cup sugar
- 1 tablespoon dark rum
- 2 tablespoons chopped dried cherries
- 2 tablespoons chopped dried pineapple
- 2 tablespoons chopped dried apricots

Instructions

1. Preheat oven to 350°F.

2. Cream butter and sugar, then add egg and vanilla.

3. Combine dry ingredients in a small bowl.

4. Add half of the dry ingredients, then the yogurt, then remaining dry ingredients.

5. Bake in a loaf pan for 35 minutes. Cool completely.

6. While cake is cooking, place nuts on a baking sheet and toast for 10 minutes.

7. Whisk cream, sugar, and rum until stiff peaks form.

8. Cut cake into cubes. In serving glasses, layer cake, rum cream, and dried fruits and nuts. Refrigerate for at least 1 hour before serving.

Almond Cherry Chocolate Bark

Ingredients

- 3/4 cup whole skin-on almonds
- 12 ounces dark chocolate (60 percent to 70 percent cocoa)
- 1/2 teaspoon pure vanilla extract
- toasted almonds
- 1/3 cup dried tart cherries, chopped

Instructions

1. Preheat oven to 350°F
2. Toast almonds until fragrant and light gold, 8 to 10 minutes.
3. Meanwhile, place 10 ounces of chocolate in a double boiler. Stir until smooth. Remove bowl from saucepan; add another 2 ounces dark chocolate and stir until smooth. Add pure vanilla extract, toasted almonds, and 1/3 cup dried tart cherries.
4. Pour onto cold baking sheet in an even layer. Refrigerate at least 1 hour.
5. Break into pieces.

Hot Chocolate Affogato with Peppermint Ice Cream

Ingredients

- 3 cups whole milk
- 1 cup chilled heavy cream, divided
- 1/3 cup sugar
- 1 large pinch of kosher salt
- 1 vanilla bean, split lengthwise
- 5 ounces semisweet or bittersweet chocolate, chopped
- 1/3 cup (loosely packed) natural unsweetened cocoa powder
- 1 tablespoon finely ground espresso or dark-roast coffee beans
- 2 pints peppermint or mint chip ice cream
- 8 small candy canes (optional)

Instructions

1. Combine milk, ½ cup cream, sugar, salt, vanilla bean, and ¼ cup water in a saucepan. Bring to a boil until sugar is dissolved. Add chocolate and cocoa powder, whisk just until mixture comes to a boil. Remove vanilla bean and blend until light and foamy. Set aside.

2. Whisk remaining ½ cup cream and coffee until stiff peaks form.

3. Scoop ice cream into small serving dishes. Pour hot cocoa over ice cream, then top with coffee whipped cream. Garnish with a small candy cane.

Thank you

Remember to grab your five full meal plans, complete with shopping lists. Each are designed with complementary food and drink from the beginning to the end, so you can't go wrong.

Meals Plans and Shopping Lists

I hope you enjoyed Christmas Recipes Made Easy.

If so, would you please take just a moment to leave a quick review of the book? This helps others find these recipes for their holiday meals.

CPSIA information can be obtained
at www.ICGtesting.com
Printed in the USA
LVHW051432271120
672814LV00016B/584

9 781989 891964